My Calling,
As I Call It!

My Calling,
As I Call It!

A journey into the life and death experiences
of patients in an ICU as seen through
the eyes of a nurse.

CLETA CRANFORD

XULON PRESS

Xulon Press Elite
2301 Lucien Way #415
Maitland, FL 32751
407.339.4217
www.xulonpress.com

Paperback ISBN-13: 978-1-6628-1764-9
Ebook ISBN-13: 978-1-6628-1765-6

Contents

Foreword

For Cleta Cranford's book, *My Calling,
As I Call It,*

by Gail Williamson.

I am honored to be able to introduce my friend and author of *My Calling, As I Call It* to you. I am a retired high school English teacher, who taught for 45 years. I, too, am a writer and have published short fiction, as well as poetry. I am currently working on a poetry book about Greek Mythology and my first novel. I served on the board of the NC Poetry Society as the Workshop Chair for eight years, and have been one of three judges for the Carl Sandburg National Poetry Contest for the last decade.

Cleta has often shared her stories about working with trauma cases, as well as patients hovering between life and death. As she relieved these experiences with me and others, it was easy to see that she loved her work as a nurse, as well as being a Christian witness to her patients. Her voice – soft and southern – can almost be heard on the page as she relates the stories that not only paint her personality for the reader, but emphasize her values, as well. Reading it brought laughter and tears and amazement as to the ease that she handled the pressures of nursing – especially nursing in critical care. I was deeply inspired, as well, to reach out to others for Christ as she has done throughout her career.

I believe she initially began the book with an idea of offering young nurses advice from her career, but her Christian *calling* could not be separated into another chapter; she found she must incorporate the two.

When it Started

Everyone has a story to tell. I suppose I am no different. It is just that I have more than ever to write since I have retired from years of nursing. Writing has never been my forte considering language arts has been one of my weaker assets. I have to say, this has been enjoyable and definitely challenging. Perhaps it is because I have been around for many years and enjoy looking back upon my life. I now realize my Christian Faith had an important impact both upon my calling as a nurse and as a Christian.

Now why would I spend time writing this? I would certainly recommend writing before this time in life and while the mental acuity is still intact. I tried to remember the details as accurately as possible: some of them are etched in the brain and others are not so much even with the help of my journals. Of course, the circumstances and names have been changed to protect the privacy of the patients.

As long as I can remember, I have been a nurse in some sort of capacity. As a farm girl, I have had plenty of opportunities to care for sick or injured animals. Whether it was being at the birth of kittens or at the difficult birth of a calf, I want to be there. Then there was the winter excitement - hog killing time. I was fully grown before I knew what a messy endeavor that was! I suppose nursing was just a continuation of my curiosity.

In nursing school I watched autopsies every Friday evening until the pathology department closed. That is the easiest way to learn anatomy and physiology. The pathologists were great teachers and much less intimidating than the instructors. Plus, they did not give exams!

The nursing profession has offered me the best of two worlds. Meeting the patient's physical needs for wellness, and at the same time, meeting the patient's psychosocial needs as a human being can be challenging, but greatly rewarding. The wear and tear on the body is one of the downsides, not to mention exposure to all kinds of pathogens.

Also, patients rarely tell you when they are going to fall. Good body mechanics are practiced, but it is the unexpected movement that can catch you off guard. I have always had the notion that the statement, "Don't worry nurse, I'm not going to fall," is a sure indication that he/she will fall! Occasionally, I would find myself on the floor with the patient on top of me before I realized what happened. At least, I broke his/her fall on the way down!

Although hospitals are more aware of the spread of infectious diseases, it does cause concern to the caretakers. Sometimes the patient's illness is known, but most of the time it is yet to be determined. It is the not knowing until it's too late to protect oneself from infectious disease that causes concern for the nurse and his/her family. Treating all patients as if they are infectious has been the greatest protection for caregivers. In the past, we did not have all the personal protection equipment that is available today.

Recently more attention has been given to the problem of assault on medical healthcare workers. According to Occupational Safety and Health Administration, incidents of serious workplace violence are four times more common in health care than in private industry *(Preventing Workplace Violence)*. As our society becomes more hostile with untreated mental illness, and mind altering drug dependence, we see some disturbing behaviors in patients and families. De-escalation of a violent situation is a skill and definitely a challenge to the health care providers.

Some years ago two chemically impaired and angry brothers threatened a male assistant and me with billy clubs. The patient's mother and sister were attempting to calm the angry brothers but they were beyond reasoning. The male assistant and I were called out of the unit to the hallway where the disturbance was taking place.The accusations were irrational and irritating to me because we were trying to keep their younger brother alive! The brothers pushed us against the wall with their billy sticks in hand, demanding loudly, "We are going to beat you up and Bubba is going with us." What could we do? Their demands grew louder and louder in the hallway which probably frightened our other patients. We were only trying to protect their seriously ill, semi-conscious younger brother from them.

Realizing our backs were against the wall literally, I could not think what to do. Then I noticed the two brothers wore glasses. "I will be glad to hold your glasses for you," I said sheepishly. The two brothers stopped the yelling and looked at me as if I had thrown ice water in their faces. My ridiculous statement had caught them off guard and de-escalated the hostile situation without my knowing it! They slammed their billy sticks back in their belt holders, cursed me, and left. By now the security guard and others had arrived to help. Hearing the details of the incident, they couldn't stop laughing. I learned an important lesson that night; do not allow yourself to ever get backed into a wall!

Another incident occurred many years ago while working the night shift. My patient was a delusional, combative lady that accused me of "running around" with her husband. The insinuation was totally ridiculous as she was so old. I was in my early 20's and she was in her late 40's! Understandably, her behavior was due to a chemical imbalance in her body. She was standing in her bed yelling accusations at me while I was trying to calm her.

Later, I thought I had succeeded in calming her. Suddenly out of nowhere, she punched me in the face, so hard it knocked me across the room, over a table and into the wall. All I remember was sliding down the wall. The noise caused the male assistant to come, who restrained her and helped stop my bleeding, broken nose. Lesson learned, never trust or get too close to a delusional, combative female patient with an "old husband!"

Once while trying to sedate a man in DTs (delusional tremors) from alcohol withdrawal, the man became so combative his sons could not calm him. Only his fractured, splinted femur kept him in the bed. Since he had an IV on the opposite side of the bed near the wall, my plan was to raise the bed, crawl under the bed, get to the IV line and give him a sedative.

It sounded like a great plan! His sons agreed and were to distract him while I tried to medicate him. His kicking and flailing slowed some and I proceeded with my plan. Crawling under the bed to access his IV, I thought he did not see me. Just as I had finished injecting the medicine, I felt a pitcher of ice and water being dumped on my head. Who knew he knew I was under his bed! Slowly the medicine calmed him. The family was so apologetic. I assured the family I was all right. Later, we had a good laugh.

Most of my career was spent in critical care nursing. In retrospect, I was an "adrenaline junkie". Rarely were we bored. The balance between making a difference in someone's life and the excitement of the impromptu emergencies describes critical care nursing.

Being away from active nursing, I seem to have a clearer idea of what it requires and its impact on the nurse and caregivers. My advice to the new nurse would be to enjoy your **calling**. Pray every day before meeting your patients. Keep your sense of humor, remain loving and kind, but firm with your patient and their families. You will make a real difference in the lives of many. Take good care of yourself; get plenty of sleep; learn to relax; learn to have fun, exercise, and you already know how to eat healthy; just do it!

Never lose sight of the **calling**. When the patient overcomes the illness or accident, it is easy to keep the calling in perspective. But what about the times when the outcomes were less than desirable? When I could not handle the pressures, I would remind myself that I was where the Lord wanted me to be. I know I was not the smartest, most efficient or the swiftest nurse available to care for the sick, but that is where God called me to be. To be there for the final minutes of someone's life is an honorable and sobering event. Dealing with the emotions surrounding the friends and families of the deceased can be an emotional drain. Keep the **calling** in mind! Death may only come once during your shift or death may present itself multiple times during a single shift! Earlier in my career, I worked in the Emergency Department and knew this all too well. I have always thought there should be some kind of deprograming available for nurses in these cases.

Developing meaningful relationships with other nurses and caretakers will be necessary to help during these emotional events. We rely on each other in stressful times more than we think we do! I cherish all who have a part in my emotional, educational, and development as a nurse. Also, develop relationships with others who are not involved in healthcare! Balance is key to your mental health. Here I must express my gratitude to my dear husband and family for their love and support.

Whatever your **calling** may be, do it as unto the Lord. If you have committed your life to the Lord Jesus, He has a plan for you. Jeremiah 29:11 is a familiar scripture: "For I know the plans I have for you" declares the Lord, "plans to prosper you and not to harm you, plans to give you hope and a future." God does not make mistakes! It is comforting to know He has you where He wants you to be.

We may have several *callings* and different *callings* at different times during our lives. The value to your *calling* is determined by your Creator. If He calls us, He will enable us to do the job. This takes the worry and concern out of the equation if we hold up our end of the bargain. My greatest *calling* is to be a follower of Jesus, a wife, mother and now a grandmother to eight amazing grandchildren along with the *calling* to nursing!

It took several years to realize how stressful my job was and how it had trained me to react differently. I was teaching critical care courses and had moved to the Education Department. I was sitting in a meeting where staff members were upset because their plan was not going as scheduled. They needed a few more volunteers to staff an upcoming community outreach. I was not very sensitive to their dilemma. "My goodness, no one is going to be hurt or die," I thought to myself. Then I realized how working in Critical Care had changed my perspective on life! I had some adjustments to make to live in the more normal world. The Educational staff were very gracious with me.

When our little daughter was in elementary school, she was asked by her teacher to stand and tell her name and something about her parents. "My daddy is a pharmacist and my momma is a nurse." When she sat down a little boy said, "Wow, that would be so neat. When you get sick your mom will wait on you and you can eat all the ice cream you want." She retorted, "My mama thinks you have to have a heart attack or stroke or you are not really sick!" Her teacher thought it was so amusing she called to tell me. Did I really seem so insensitive to our children when they were sick? Probably, I did.

Healthcare providers just as any other profession must be on guard for signs and symptoms of impending burnout. Feelings of being overwhelmed, helpless, resentful, or cynical of others are some signs of burnout. Managing prolonged stress and creating renewed interest in the work does wonders. Recognizing these symptoms and taking steps to alleviate them may be as simple as taking a much needed vacation.

Other colleagues will from time to time struggle with burnout. It is difficult not to become influenced by the attitude of others. Be aware of negativity; it is a destructive force. Learn to recognize it and avoid negativity at all cost. It is like swimming against the tide when the atmosphere becomes infected with negativity. Keep a positive attitude and you may be able to help turn the negative tide to a positive atmosphere. Encourage fellow colleagues whenever possible and you too will be encouraged.

My husband has helped me to keep a proper perspective in this area by insisting on taking a vacation even though I feel I do not need it. After about two days into the vacation, I realized how much I really needed it. I have also learned to see my **calling** as being just that. It adds so much value to nursing to be able to do it as unto the Lord and allowing Him take control of the problems. He always does a better job than I could do, and the stress and anxiety is lessened.

The physical and emotional demands may lead to exhaustion and mental fatigue associated with burn out. Dangerous mistakes may be made as a result. Errors in treatments or in medications could cause damage to the patient's wellbeing. Yes, I have made mistakes. Thank the Lord, none of my mistakes caused harm to the patient.

Learn from your mistakes; why was it made; forgive yourself and move forward, or burnout will be hounding you. Dwelling on the mistake gives energy to it and may cause you to make an even greater mistake!

So, admit to the mistake without making excuses. There is nothing like being held accountable for your mistakes to crush the false pride that develops when we deny or blame others for our mistakes. Blaming others leads to denial, prevents maturity, and a teachable spirit. Use the built in safety standards, precautionary measures, checks, and balances, provided by the institution to prevent making mistakes. No short cuts! These steps and regulations are provided for the purpose of preventing errors.

Medicine changes daily. Keeping up with the progress in diagnosing and treatments is a challenging, but rewarding endeavor. As we give certain medications that are very dangerous which require close monitoring during administration, we need to be able to be focused and attentive. While being attentive to what we are doing, we must appear to be calm and reassuring to the patient so as not to elicit his/her fear and anxiety. Always keep the patient's well-being first. Embrace the changes in medicine, keep learning, while knowing your limitations and staying in touch with your values will serve for your own mental well-being.

On the cutting edge of research is the development of precision medicine. Information from genes, proteins, and environment is tailored for the individual's health (Collins, Heather, Calro, Sherri, Morrison, Stephanie. *Precision Medicine).* Technology, with its physics and biology may be useful in the future along with new drugs for treatment. The use of low voltage electric fields to treat aggressive cancers just received FDA approval (Hsieh, Chih Hsiung. *Application).* Sound waves impact on the body are being explored and questioned. Cell physiology has been revolutionized by understanding that our body's cells communicate with each other, form memories, and cause specific reactions in order to preserve the health of the body. While this is excellent if timed correctly, the rapid over reaction poses problems. For example, a Covid 19 infection in certain individuals may cause an overreaction of the autoimmune system creating a cytokine storm. Regulating these reactions is a challenge. We are beginning to learn the importance of maintaining cellular balance to keep the whole organism balanced. The energy and light within the cell are being traced and measured (*Using*

Sound). Research is revealing new mysteries everyday about the human body.

To quote my nurse friend Mary, "Nurses are the first to open the eyes of the infant and the last to close the eyes in death." The thrill of seeing a new life begin, being instrumental in helping to save a life, or helping someone to transition from this life to the next results in a plethora of deep emotions.

Metamorphosis of
the Calling

In the following stories, I have tried to share some of my experiences as an ICU nurse. The first experience I had with a Near Death Experience occurred in the late sixties. At first, very little was known or discussed about Near Death Experiences. In fact, we called it "out of the body experience" if it were mentioned at all.

The religious community was slow to embrace the Near Death Experiences. Some said it was a deception of Satan to deceive people into thinking "everyone was going to heaven." True, Satan is known for perverting God's plans and purposes. Some of the experiences I've read about do seem to be just that. But how does one explain the Near Death Experiences that were not at all heavenly? And how about children reporting seeing things they were unaware of before the experience?

Now there are a plethora of stories of Near Death Experiences. Some of them do refer to children. The most astounding story I have heard about was a young boy who had left his body during a medical emergency. The boy and his Dad were on a TV talk show telling about the Near Death Experience of the child. The boy asked his parents about his sister he met while in heaven. The shocked parents had never told him about the child they had lost earlier during a pregnancy. Apparently, the child was not "lost" after all. She was alive in heaven!

In the Book of Acts, at the end of chapter 7, we are told about Stephen while he was being stoned to death. Stephen had just given a great testimony about Jesus being the Son of God to the established Jewish leaders. The leaders became so enraged, they dragged him out and began stoning him. Verse 55: "But Stephen, full of the Holy Spirit, looked up to heaven and saw the glory of God, and Jesus standing at the right hand of God." He was looking into heaven, seeing Jesus himself. Jesus had been seated but stood up to meet him! What did Stephen do? He prayed for the stoners! Verse 60-b: "Lord, do not hold this sin against them." That is ultimate in human forgiveness!

It would definitely take the grace of God to react in such an impressive manner as Stephen did! Saul, later known as Paul, was holding the stoners' coats for the event and he was impressed by Stephen, although it took him a while to process all he saw and heard that day. After Paul's conversion on the road to Damascus, in the Acts of the Apostles, chapter 9: he tells the incident and his involvement in persecution of the early church and how he had received God's forgiveness for himself: God's ultimate forgivenesses!

In 2 Corinthians, chapter 12:1-5: the apostle Paul relates this experience of a man (referring to himself) in Christ who was caught up to the third heaven. "Whether it was in the body or apart from the body I do not know, but God knows - was caught up into paradise. He heard inexpressible things, things that man is not permitted to tell."

Yes, I do believe the episodes that are described here, but I also know that Satan can mimic God's miracles. I can attest to individuals who have had a Near Death Experience radiating such peace and calmness. Satan cannot mimic that same kind of peace and calmness! Let us weigh all the circumstances against the Word of God. Does it line up with the teachings of God, does it give glory to Him, and does it build faith in the believer? Without the production of fruit, there is no validity to the experience.

James 1:2-4 reminds us:
"My brethren, count it all joy when you fall into various trials, knowing that the testing of your faith produces patience. But let patience have its perfect work, that you may be perfect and complete, lacking nothing."

Hebrews 13:21 NLT:
May he equip you with all you need for doing his will. May he produce in you through the power of Jesus Christ, every good thing that is pleasing to him. All glory to him forever and amen!

Romans 11:29 NLT:

For God's gifts and call can never be withdrawn.

"I Will Be Back!"

"Never will I leave you; never will I forsake you." Hebrews 13:5.

Mr. Mallard:

It was late Saturday evening when we admitted Mr. Mallard, a man in his late 50's, to ICU with chest pain, to rule out myocardial infarction. Since I had already reported off on my patients, I was helping to get Mr. Mallard's admission completed. I know patients get tired of the multiple questions we ask but we have to take a good, thorough history and physical. His pain was under control so I started with just the necessary questions.

Suddenly, he had a cardiac arrest! Suddenly, we were in a code! He was successfully resuscitated and we were busy getting him stabilized with medications and IV drips. Later, I asked him if he would like prayer. He quickly replied, "Yes I would." I prayed, what I don't know exactly but I included a salvation message. I did not have time to ask him if he was a Christian. Even if a person thinks he/she is a Christian, he/she may need to rededicate his/her life and it certainly will not hurt to be reminded of Christ's marvelous gift. I usually pray what the Holy Spirit impresses on me to pray. His heart rhythm was back to normal and his condition was stable.

He suddenly had another cardiac arrest! We had to defibrillate him twice to obtain a pulse. The cardiologist was reviewing the chart when the patient opened his eyes and looked at me. "Now, don't worry about me. I've seen Jesus and he told me it would happen again, but He would again send me back." My mind went blank and I had a very *spiritual* thought, "I wish Jesus would tell me that you would be coming back!"

True to his word, Mr Mallard had his third cardiac arrest! He again was resuscitated.

When it was all over and he was stable again, I found out he was a visiting evangelist. I had witnessed to a man of God! I felt a little uncomfortable with this; however, Rev. Mallard was so gracious and kind he never mentioned it.

I regret I did not go with Rev. Mallard when he gave his testimony. He had invited me to do so. These chances only come once in a while and I have always regretted I didn't go with him. Now that I am older, I understand how precious these opportunities are.

> 2 Corinthians 5: 6-8
> *"Therefore we are always confident and know that as long as we are at home in the body we are away from the Lord. We live by faith, not by sight. We are confident, I say, and would prefer to be away from the body and home with the Lord."*

Interpretation of Judging

Matthew 7:1
"Do not judge, or you too will be judged."

That scripture has a lot of interpretations and I want to give you yet another one. I thought it only meant to have a negative word or attitude about another person in judgment for their actions or deeds. I never thought it may mean something else.

Mr. Rover:

Turning off my car, I whispered my usual prayer, "Oh God, send me to someone to witness today." During the report, I assumed my prayer was answered. The patient in bed #3 was a lifelong alcoholic and was in great distress from complications due to liver failure.

He was angry, lashing out to anyone that tried to help him with derogatory and foul language. I did not say much to him except to ask him if I could do anything to make him more comfortable. He let me know and I will not share that with you.

He was hemorrhaging per rectum and required several units of blood and constant cleaning. It was all I could do to keep up with the demands. I stated my usual calming statement about how sick he was and it must be difficult to tolerate all we were having to do to him. He just looked at me for a few seconds then said bluntly, "Thank you".

Thinking this had softened his angry disposition, I thought it would be an appropriate time to witness to him. Very cautiously, lovingly and quietly, I asked if I might pray for him. "No!" he answered emphatically. I was shocked, stunned, could not believe he had said "No". After all, his life was hanging in the balance! I had never had anyone in that situation say "No" to prayer before nor since! I knew he was not rejecting me, but he was rejecting God.

When witnessing to people I don't know, I try to remember the words of Jesus in Matthew 10:16: "Therefore be as shrewd as snakes and gentle as doves." I think I simply said, "Ok". But I did pray for him silently as I administered the IV blood and medication.

Most of my time was spent with him and I did not spend much time with my other patient, Mr. Rover. Mr. Rover and his wife now in their late 60's, had devoted their life to the care of his severely mentally and physically challenged sister. Ms. Rover had just passed away leaving all the care of the sister to him. The nurses were touched with the situation and the kindness of this man. Since his condition was better, he would be moved out of the unit the next day.

My shift was about over and I noticed Mr. Rover was still awake. "Are you ok? Do you need something before I go." I said, hoping he would say "no". I was tired and wanted to just go home. Drawing closer to his bed, I noticed he looked as if he had been crying. Oh, how my heart was touched. No longer was I tired, no longer did I just think about going home.

"Mr. Rover, I am going to church tomorrow and I'm going to pray for you," I said.

"Don't wait till tomorrow, please pray for me now, please," he said, holding on to my arm, "I'm not sure I'm ready." I sensed the urgency in his voice but remembering my previous experience that night, I felt so inadequate.

Nevertheless, I began praying, "Dear Heavenly Father, we thank you for showing us your love by sending your son, Jesus, into this world so that our sin would no longer separate us from You. Jesus paid the price by being the perfect sacrifice by His death on the cruel cross for our sin. We confess and turn from our sins and ask You to please forgive us. Jesus, we believe You rose from the dead; we invite You to live in our hearts forever. Take our will and may it line up with Your will. We thank you for loving us; we receive and accept Your forgiveness as we forgive others their offenses toward us. We trust You to lead, guide, and direct our new lives in You. Thank you, Jesus, for bringing Mr. Rover through this heart attack and saving his life. Amen!" I did not think much about the prayer at that time but I do remember how grateful and peaceful he was for the prayer.

It was late, way past time to go home and I still had a thirty minute drive.

As I was preparing for bed, the phone rang. Usually it would be about something I had forgotten to do, or chart, or clarify. It was the night nurse, "What did you say to Mr. Rover? A few minutes after you left, he had a cardiac arrest. We could not resuscitate him."

"Oh my, I just prayed a salvation prayer with him, that's all," I said.

It was then I started to review the evening's happenings. He must have sensed what was about to occur. Was that why his prayer request was so urgent? What if I had missed the chance to pray with him? My prayer was answered after all! I tried to help God out by taking it on myself to know who was in need of prayer. I missed it! I judged the alcoholic as needing Jesus and I judged Mr. Rover, a kind, loving man to be righteous, and not needing prayer. Only God knows the heart. There are probably a number of individuals who live exemplary lives who have never known what it is to know Jesus Christ on a personal level. We may mistake this knowing about Jesus rather than really knowing Jesus personally.

We then start trying to please God by our good works instead of trusting His free gift of salvation. We cannot earn God's love by our works.

Matthew 7:22
"Many will say to me on that day, 'Lord, Lord did we not prophesy in your name, and in your name drive out demons and perform many miracles?' Then I will tell then plainly I never knew you. Away from me, you evil doer.

I Do Not Know

How do we explain out of body experience or Near Death Experiences? As I have said we were told it was simply hallucinations, delusions, or oxygen deprivation that were the causative factor. In a controlled situation like a hospital setting, keeping the oxygen level at a more functional level is possible through quality CPR and oxygen delivery systems for a short duration. Of course, the type of injury or disease process would dictate whether this could be possible or not. Most codes happen so quickly there is not time to medicate them with sedation nor would this be our goal in an emergency situation. None of the patients I encountered were given to delusions or hallucinations before or after the experience.

Just as life holds its own experiences, death holds its own experiences. Keep in mind, death is only a transition.

Most of the patients describe a similar visual and verbal experience. Most report hovering high above their body, having no pain, and seeing the activities in detail going around their bodies. This does not seem to cause concern or anxiousness. One individual reported seeing a healthcare worker drop a pen on the floor, but he was unable to find it. The pen had rolled under another stretcher. Upon his return to his body he told the worker where the pen was. The pen was found exactly where he said it was!

Some other similarities is being transported through time and space at a rapid speed through something like a tunnel to the other side. The colors they see are intriguing, no words to describe, and colors not present here on earth. The flowers are alive, so beautiful and are everywhere. One dear man said it seemed as if the flowers were singing and stepping on them had no effect on their beauty. Beyond the beauty, the peace and permeating love consumes the whole being related to another. Most report they have a choice about returning to their physical bodies. The return is similar to the exit, hovering over the body before entrance. Once inside their body, they feel pain, especially if trauma is present, or discomfort if disease is present. I had an end stage cancer patient talking incomprehensibly to me, smile, and then open his eyes, look around, and said "Oh, I am back here again!" I just smiled as we had previously discussed these trips to Heaven. I have noticed one thing they all have in common; **death holds no fear or dread for them.** They seem to have more zest for living but no longer are anxious about death.

Why are Near Death Experiences happening now? That, I do not know. Could it be we are entering the last days when there is an increase of spiritual activity on the earth? God has always given His people what is needed to finish the race in any certain period of time. Yes, with the increase in demonic activities, God is allowing His own children to experience an increase in Spiritual experiences. One thing I do know, God has said, "Never will I leave you; never will I forsake you." So we say with confidence, "The Lord is my helper; I will not be afraid. What can man do to me?" Hebrews 13:5b&6. "So (as the result of the Messiah's intervention) they shall (reverently) fear the name of the Lord from the west, and His glory from the rising of the sun. When the enemy shall come in like a flood, the Spirit of the Lord will lift up a standard against him and put him to flight (for He will come like a rushing stream which breath of the Lord drives)." Isaiah 59:19 AMP. Are these happenings part of the reassurance that God is with us who believe, and will take care of us, no matter what happens. I think so!

Human secularism denies God and His ability to help man with the complexities of life. Man becomes the center of his life or an idol unto himself. Therefore, they are deficient in knowing and understanding the aspects of the created being. Yes, they may agree that we have a body with a brain and an emotional system, but they have no knowledge of man's spirit and God's transformational power on the spirit of man. One-third of their personhood is missing! Public education, secular colleges, and universities have not afforded the students complete knowledge of just who they were created to be. How can this generation be expected to know who they are and that they can control their impulses? How can they know that God loves them and wants to change their life by His Spirit? The greater question is; how can we bring education to this uninformed generation? This was not so in the beginning of our educational system, but the secular ideology crept in with their teachings of evolution, denying God, and making man the center of his universe. However, a few religious institutions have held to the teachings of God and are making a positive impact on society and these students will be needed as our society becomes more neurotic and self-absorbed.

As he usually does, man tries to find answers devoid of God within himself for his dilemmas. Psychology opens the door to understanding the mind and emotions from a human standpoint and the resultant behaviors, but gives no real answers as to how to change the heart. While psychology can give us labels for classes of behaviors both normal and abnormal, it falls short when it comes to providing permanent solutions to the behaviors. Oh yes, we have a plethora of drugs to mask symptoms by replacing or calming down certain neurotransmitters and hormones, but none that eliminate the root cause of the problem.

Since God and His teachings have been removed from most of our institutions, we have eliminated at least one third or more of our understanding and knowledge into the human being. In the past, we have relied on the family or church's teachings to counteract the secular teaching. With the breakdown of the nuclear family, it appears the families are unreliable to deliver this much needed instruction. Sadly, secularism has invaded the church's once held morals to the degree that differences between the world and church seem negligible. We major on what the emotional and physical body requires of us, and ignore the spiritual need. Movies and TV programs major in "feelings" and other ways of playing on our emotions to get most out of the ratings. Those most gullible to this false or slanted ideology are the younger population who did not live through the historical event. Often when confronted with the truth, it is met with much skepticism.

An Angel?

James 5:15
"And a prayer offered in faith will make the sick person well; the Lord will raise him up."

Mr. Bair:

We never know when we will be called upon to be a part of someone else's life, or death! God has a habit of showing up when we least expect it turning the mundane into the miraculous to serve His purpose. That is what makes it so exciting to serve Him.

Mr. Bair, a middle aged man, was preparing to be transferred to the step down unit. His multiple lines had been reduced to one or two. Everything was going as planned. He was happy he had survived ICU! His nurse was preparing to get him up in a chair for transfer since his condition was so stable.

Now, in a real ICU, an emergency is not like as seen on TV. We try to avoid panic at all cost by not yelling or screaming but calling for help in a distinct, audible, firm tone that is well known by the other nurses. Suddenly, I heard my name called in that emergency tone.

Mr. Bair was in a full cardiac code in seconds. His pulseless body fell back into the bed. The head of the bed was lowered, a nurse was doing compressions, the respiratory therapist was delivering oxygen by a bag-valve-mask. We defibrillated him three times, reassessed, but the ventricular fibrillation continued. Medications to treat the short run of ventricular tachycardia and then ventricular fibrillation were given. The code protocol of defibrillation, assessment, medication and CPR continued. A cardiologist was soon at the bedside to direct the code. An endotracheal tube was placed to deliver oxygen more effectively. Many labs and arterial blood gases were drawn to try to determine the reason for the continued arrest. It was determined the most likely reason was a pulmonary embolism. (A condition in which a blood clot travels to the pulmonary artery, occluding the artery thus preventing blood from entering the lungs and then the heart.) After about 40 minutes of defibrillation, medication, and CPR, the rhythm changed from ventricular fibrillation to a flat line. A final blood gas report came back. I don't know why I remember this but the PaO2 was 19! This test shows the oxygen level in the arterial blood which is normally 75-100. The physician stopped the code and pronounced the patient dead.

Another person and I were discontinuing the endotracheal tube, the lines, and preparing the body. All of a sudden, I was standing over his body and I heard myself say out loud, "Live, don't die!" Did I say that? That was the first time I heard that statement was after I said it! But God heard it! And live he did! He was alive!

I did not see Mr. Bair for approximately 18 years. He was then readmitted to the ICU and I went to see him. I asked him if he knew me. In a polite manner he replied "Your face seems familiar."

"I was with you in ICU when you were very sick several years ago," I said cautiously.

"Oh yes, I do remember. That's when my heart stopped beating," was his reply.

"Do you remember I was standing by your bed and said, 'Live, don't die?'" He looked at me grinning.

"Was that you? I thought an angel said that." Now I was laughing.

"I can assure you I am **not** an angel! We all had a good laugh.

Turning to his wife, I asked her if she and the family were there that day. "Yes, and we were all praying for God to heal him and He did!" The family had been told of the change in his condition that day and they went to God immediately with their request.

So that was it! It was their request to God that bypassed my brain, into my spirit and out of my mouth it came. I can not, nor do I want to take credit for that! I can tell you that I did not even think of that statement. And if I had thought of it, I would probably not have said it. It had not been fully revealed to me at that time the authority of the believer and the power of the spoken word.

As stated before, words are so powerful for good or for evil. After all, the earth was spoken into existence with words, "Light be," as the Hebrew interprets the text, and so it was. Later the sun, moon, stars, animals and all living creatures came into existence via the spoken word. Only man was created and later woman was taken from his side. They were created, formed from the dust of the earth and the Lord breathed into them the breath of life. Genesis 1.

The beginning of James chapter 3, talks a lot about the tongue and its unruliness. "All kinds of animals, birds, reptiles and creatures of the sea are being tamed and have been tamed by man, but no man can tame the tongue." James 3:7. No man can, but Jesus can help us tame this unruly part of our being! The problem is not the physical muscle of our body, the tongue, but the heart. We can close our mouth, stop our larynx from vibrating, control the flow of words, but yet, we choose not to do it! Why? When our emotions are not controlled by the Holy Spirit, these raw emotions erupt with rage, wanting to get our two cents in, wanting to hurt others with words, bragging to make ourselves look important, or simply chattering. Jesus's healing in these areas gets to the root of the problem, the heart. The heart submitted to God can speak these positive, uplifting words, and slowly the tongue will comply. That is the power of the spoken word. For good, for evil, we get to choose. Proverbs 18:21: "The tongue has the power of life and death, and those who love it will eat its fruit."

No Fear, Just Peace!

Psalm 23:4 KJV.
"Yea, though I walk through the valley of the shadow of death, I will fear no evil: for thou art with me."

Mr. Lamb:

On a rare occasion, I would work on the step down unit. I entered my first patient's room, Mr. Lamb, and introduced myself. Although he was in his early 70's, he looked much younger. He looked at me for a few seconds and then he said, "When you get a spare minute, I must talk to you." I sensed this was a God appointment and I needed to be able to listen.

"Ok, when I get my rounds completed, I will be back."

Later, I was listening to Mr Lamb's experience. "Several days ago I was in the Emergency Room with terrible chest pain and I was having trouble breathing. I felt myself leave my body and then I hovered above it. I could see everybody working on my body and I saw you pull out a stool and stand on it so you could push on my chest. Then, I left the room and was taken into the most beautiful, warm place. The colors were so brilliant, colors I have never seen before and the flowers were beyond description in beauty and they were singing! I knew I was in heaven! I sensed there was a guide beside me although I never saw him. Such love and warmth I had never felt before. Then I saw Jesus in all His glory. I fell down! The light was so bright around Him I could barely see. Jesus turned and said to someone beside Him, 'This is Mr. Lamb. He has one request to see his sons come to faith in Me before he comes home.' As quickly as Jesus said that I felt myself propelled backwards through the atmosphere and I re-entered my body."

I knew the nurse was not me as I had not worked the ED in several weeks. After reassuring him I believed his story because I had heard a few stories like that from patients who were having a Near Death Experience. He was quite relieved and surprised to hear it had happened to others. "I don't believe that it was me that was in the Emergency Room," I said.

"Well if it was not you then it was your twin. She pulled the stool from under the other bed and stood on it so she could push on my chest." I was amazed he told the incident with such detail and I also knew there was a nurse in the Emergency Department that resembled me. Before I left him that evening, I wanted to know what he planned to do next.

Apparently, Mr. Lamb had already thought of that, "I want to tell my boys what happened, but I am afraid. They are both driving in tomorrow."

After a brief pause I said, "Would you like me to be with you when you tell them?"

"Oh yes, I would!" he replied.

Mr. Lamb had received Jesus into his heart later in life. He had never told his sons about Jesus's salvation plan. He was unsure how they would respond. Although he felt compelled to tell his sons, he was still hesitant. Over a week had passed before he had the courage to tell me. I encouraged him and believed with him that the Lord would give him the right words to say.

The following day, the two "boys" were already visiting Mr. Lamb when I arrived. They were two very well dressed, polite men, not what I expected. After greetings and handshakes, the four of us sat down and I said, "Mr. Lamb has something interesting to tell you." He told his miraculous story to his sons with the same details. I could not tell from their reaction what they were thinking. Mr. Lamb was discharged the next day. I did not see him again.

Sometime months later, we came home after being at the lake a few days. Our phone was ringing. "Where have you been? We've been trying to contact you. We had a former patient of yours who said he must talk to you. He never told us what it was about, he just kept asking for you."

"What was his name." It was Mr. Lamb. The nurse went on to tell me what was wrong with him and how he died.

How I regretted I had not been there to hear what he had to tell me. We did not have a landline at our cabin and that was long before cell phones.

Two weeks later, I received a letter from Mr. Lamb! His family was cleaning off his desk and found a typewritten page about his miraculous journey. He had used the page when he gave a testimony at his church. Around the edge was a handwritten note from Mr Lamb to me. He had seen the salvation of his sons and wanted me to know. The family thought I would like to know and right they were! God is so good!

I Corinthians 2:9
However, as it is written:
"No eye has seen, no ear has heard, no mind has conceived what God has prepared for those who love him".

The Spirit

Jesus said:

"I am the door, by me if any man enters he shall be saved...come into me and I will give you rest. John 10:9 KJV

"May your whole spirit, soul and body be kept blameless at the coming of our Lord Jesus Christ." 1 Thessalonians 5:23. The Spirit is the conduit which allows us to communicate with God. "And if the Spirit of Him Who raised up Jesus from the dead dwells in you, [then] He Who raised up Christ Jesus from the dead will also restore to life your mortal (short-lived, perishable) bodies through His Spirit Who dwells in you." Romans 8:11 AMP.

First of all, we are a spirit, we possess a soul, and we live in a body. The spirit man began whenever God breathed in Adam's nostrils the breath of life making him an eternal spiritual being, never to die! God's desire was to have a people with which He could share intimate fellowship and to love unconditionally. His creation had to have the freedom to choose to love Him or not. How else could we have true fellowship with Him unless we were free to love Him or not to love Him? He did not create robots. He knew we would rebel against His plan, but He did it anyway. Why? I think it may be somewhat like how my husband and I felt before we had children. We knew they might break our hearts but our love and desire for them even before they were conceived was so intense it overpowered our concerns. And that intense love has not disappointed us!

Adam's physical body lived 930 years after the fall, but his Spirit that once had perfect communion with God's Spirit was now dead. Adam was now left with only his human spirit. This loss left a God shaped vacuum within the spirit that only God's Spirit can fill. Oh yes, we keep trying to fill that vacuum with many possessions, power, money, entertainment, other people, places, education, titles, to name a few. All the while, the precious communion, fellowship, and intimacy with our Father is all we need to feel fulfilled, joyful, and content. The once marvelous plan for intimacy between man and God, so marvelous it was, it took that free moral agent to mess it up!

So we lost that precious, satisfying communication with the Father after the fall. We may try to establish communion with God by with our good deeds, good works, and keeping the Commandments that God gave us. Try as we will, we can not reach the righteous perfection required by the Law. The Law could only tell us what we should and should not do, but the law lacks the ability to help us obey the law in our heart. Our spirit is still dead to God's Spirit! We needed a savior to save ourselves from ourselves. This is what Isaiah said in 64:6 about our efforts to reach God: "All of us have become like one who is unclean, all *our* righteous acts are like filthy rags." But our God had a plan!

Suddenly, after the fall, Adam and Eve knew they were wrong, felt alienated from God, knew guilt, made excuses, became fearful, and hid from God. Genesis 3 tells this story and also unveils God's future plan of redemption of mankind. God said to Satan in verse 15: "And I will put enmity between you and the woman, and between your offspring and her Offspring; He (Jesus) will bruise and tread your head underfoot, and you will lie in wait and bruise His heel." Amp. This refers to the miraculous Offspring of the virgin woman, Mary, who is Jesus. Jesus's life and death on the cross resulted in His victorious reign over Satan, death and the grave. This marvelous plan was to rebirth our dead, sinful spirit so we could once again commune with our Father! In His unconditional love for us, God gave His only son Jesus to be the perfect blood sacrifice for the sin that separated us from our Father. In times past, sacrifices of animals just covered sin; Jesus's blood now removes sin as far as the East is from the West!

In the temple, the 30 foot high veil which separated God from man was torn from top to bottom at the death of Jesus on the cross! This signified God had intervened; the veil was too high and thick for man to tear from top to bottom. Now, mankind has direct access himself to communion with God, if he chooses to do so! Jesus's death on the cross not only provides salvation but it gives us a new spirit to commune with the Father. Finally, our spirit could be alive once again to God. "God is Spirit, and His worshippers must worship in spirit and truth." Jesus states in John 4:24.

After His resurrection, Jesus appeared to His followers several times in a forty day period. On one occasion He commanded, "Do not leave Jerusalem, but wait for the gift my Father promised which you have heard me speak about. For John baptized with water, but in a few days you will be baptized with the Holy Spirit." Acts 1:4b&5. Their bodies, soul, and spirits were going to be baptized into the Holy Spirit by Jesus! This was possible because Jesus had returned to the Father and then sent the third person of the Godhead, Holy Spirit to live in us. The Holy Spirit is a person who is a comforter, healer, teacher, leader, helper, friend, and an advocate who intercedes for us.

In Genesis 2:16&17, we are told: And the Lord God commanded the man, "You are free to eat from any tree in the garden; but you must not eat from the tree of the knowledge of good and evil, for when you eat of it you will surely die." Eve, being deceived by Satan, saw it was good, ate the fruit for the forbidden tree, and gave it to Adam to eat. It makes perfect sense for us to not know what evil is because we, in the natural, see evil as enticing, inviting, or mysterious. It piques our insatiable curiosity. Ask any parent of a two year old. It is that which is forbidden that makes it so appealing. We call it human nature.

In the beginning, why the knowledge of "good" is forbidden is perplexing. It seems as if we need to be able to truly identify what is "good." Perhaps God knew we would define *"good"* according to our own selfish desires or human intelligence. Situation ethics is a perfect example. If it feels good, then do it; there are no moral absolutes, and another example is the evolution of the species. Do I need to say, "Pro Choice?" There are so many lies our culture has told us over and over and it has caused mayhem within our society. We may justify ourselves by thinking "but, it is legal!" Man's legal laws are man's thoughts, fallible, and are subject to change. Only God's laws are immutable, contain the truth, and remain forever, can be trusted. Isaiah 5:20: "Woe to those who call evil good and good evil." Also, He did not want us to settle for "good" when He had planned the "best" for us. God had a backup plan!

In God's graciousness, He provides knowledge of good and evil through an inner voice, a God given gift, the conscience. The conscience could lead us to do what is right! So what is the problem? Remember, we have free will; we are fallen. We can choose to obey that small inner voice or not. Before the Law, mankind relied on the conscience to lead them. But that did not always turn out well. Often the voice of our conscience is ignored willingly because we want what we want, or have to compete with other voices such as overactive or prejudiced minds. Is that why the conscience is more easily heard during rest or sleep?

Our Jesus had been turned over to the Roman governor to be tried in a mock trial. Matthew 27:19 NLT: "Just then, as Pilate was sitting on the judgment seat, Pilate's wife sent him this message: 'Leave that innocent man alone. I suffered through a terrible nightmare about him last night.'" God's gift of conscience was working in her to relay information about the unjust trial and injustice to Jesus.

After refusal to obey the convicting voice of God, we dull our senses to hear and obey. Paul's first letter to Timothy describes in Chapter 1:19: "Holding on to faith and a **good conscience**. Some have rejected these and have shipwrecked their faith." And in Chapter 4: Paul states what happens if we abandon the faith and follow deceiving spirits. Verse 2: "Such teaching comes through hypocritical liars, whose consciences have been seared as with a hot iron."

Another spiritual gift the Father provides His children is a measure of faith as Romans 12:3 states: "For by the grace given me I say to every one of you: Do not think of yourself more highly than you ought, but rather think of yourself with sober judgement, in accordance with the measure of faith God has given you." Why a measure? Probably because we would blame God if we thought someone else was given more faith than we possessed! The measure is a certain amount, to be exercised to grow, to be built upon by experience, to be protected from doubt, unbelief and then be stolen by the enemy. Faith is simply taking sides with God on the issue.

The 11th Chapter of Hebrews tells of the patriots of old and how they worked the measure of faith for growth. One that stands out is Noah who built a huge boat on dry ground; he had never seen rain and yet he believed what God said about the destruction to come. And then there was Abraham's faith that caused him to continue to believe God for the promised son even in his old age. Later he offered that son Issac as a sacrifice to God. Abraham believed God would raise him from the dead because of God's promise to him about his descendants being many. God intervened, stopped the knife and Abraham passed the test of faith. They had no written Word to guide them, just faith in God's spoken word! So what is faith?

"Faith is the assurance of things hoped for, the evidence of things not seen." Hebrews 11:1. The essentials of faith is believing in your heart (spirit), making your request to God, confessing what is believed, and then act on the belief. Faith is like a muscle, it must be used to maintain functionally. Faith must be exercised to grow, tested, and tried to help us grow, and kept strong to insure our future faith walks. Faith is a *knowing* - knowing within your spirit with certainty that what you have asked God for is yours. If you are a believer, take the measure of faith **God has given you and act on it!** Faith is expecting God to do what He promises! Apply your imagination to assist in seeing it done! The first and true benefit of faith is to believe in Jesus's life, death, and resurrection to inherit eternal life and to live with Him in our heart now and forever. After believing this, we have love, joy, peace, patience, kindness, goodness, faithfulness, gentleness, and self-control available to our spirits. All these positive attributes are great influences on the health of our spirit, soul, and body. If you need to grow your measure of faith immerse yourself in the Word, because faith comes by hearing and hearing of the Word of God.

Of course our enemy has a plan to derail our faith by using his destructive tools. He tries to get us deceived by lies about God and His love. He does this by injecting doubt, disbelief, or discouragement into our thinking to form a wrong belief about God. If he is unsuccessful in confronting our faith directly, he will distract us by our negative behaviors to poison our faith. Faith blockers are failure to forgive ourselves and others, sin and rebellion to God, contention, bitterness, or pride. His favorite tool is having us uproot our own confession of faith by our words that do not line up with what God says about the situation. Watch your words! Isaiah 55:11: "So is my word that goes out from my mouth: It will not return to me empty, but accomplish what I desire and achieve the purpose for which I sent it." God sends the word; we say what He says about the situation and send the same word back to the Father, full of accomplishments and purpose! Be aware! Satan will use the spirit of fear to attack our minds and cause confusion and anxiety. We must confront these attacks by reminding Satan there is no fear in God's love; He loves us unconditionally, and has provided everything we need.

Romans 15:13: NLT: "I pray that God, the source of hope will fill you completely with joy, and peace because we trust in Him. Then you will overflow with confident hope through the power of the Holy Spirit." God is our source of hope; how could it be any other source? And in Hebrews 6:19 NLT: "This hope is a strong and trustworthy anchor for our souls. It leads us through the curtain into God's inner sanctuary." God's hope and our hope in that hope lead us to a feeling of expectancy that everything is going to be alright. Hope is not found in our circumstances or the manner in which we view our circumstances, but in knowing for certain our God will not disappoint us. Hope works within our emotional realm to prepare us to receive the good things of God. It is not a state of wishfulness, but a state of expectancy!

To quote Hal Lindsey, a person can live 4-6 weeks without food, 3-5 days without water, 10-15 minutes without oxygen, and only a few seconds without hope. Hope and faith join the mind, will, and emotions in a determination and tenacity like no other (Lindsey, *Man Can)*. "Now, these three remain: faith, hope and love. But the greatest of these is love." 1Corinthians 13:13

God is love! I remember a psychology professor stating that to mess with our young minds. He also said, "So, anything you do in love is godly." I remember feeling a "check" within my young spirit. "Not true!", I thought, but I did not know why. That statement would be true, if it represented the essence of the one true God, but the god he was referring to was of a different character than the God I knew. Perhaps he was unaware of the four or more words used to describe "love" as Greek language does. Since the English language has only one word for "love", much is lost in the interpretation of love. Whether he knew this or not, academia tends to do that to naive students. What if the "check" had not occurred? My life could have been shipwrecked! After all, I had the same temptations of any young person who was living five hundred miles away from home! This is why it is ultimately important to introduce children and young people to the deceptive ways of others and Satan. Instilling these concepts and the Word of God early give children an up on the world!

The "God kind" of love is known as *agape* in the Greek. (Other kinds of love will be discussed later.) *Agape* love is unconditional, unrelenting, and always available! We cannot do anything to deserve it, be good enough to earn it, or to be worthy enough for His love. God loves because that is the essence of who He is! God is love who loves the whole evil world! I am not sure we totally comprehend such love, but if you have committed your life to Jesus; you have tasted and have access to *agape* love. Jesus, in the Sermon on the Mount, teaches the crowd to "Love your enemies and pray for those who persecute you, that you may be the sons of your Father in heaven." Matthew 5:44&45a. Jesus was talking about *agape* love. How do we love like that? Ask the Lord for grace to love like Jesus does! Then obey willingly as He directs. This *agape* love does not require emotions, but when practiced enough we may find a desire to fulfill God's perfect will by expressing His *agape* love. *Agape* love is a spiritual gift from God. This gift is a conduit that expresses unconditional love to others. (Lewis, *Four Greek*).

Agape love is powerful, all-encompassing force which transforms, heals, makes whole, changes attitudes, releases faith, gives hope, salvation, defeats Satan, and much more. Satan has no answers or tools to use against the love of God! That is the power of God's love! The natural reaction to offense is to become offended, angry, hostile, bitter or to spread strife. We must choose to walk in God's *agape* love. Then we are capable with His help to walk in His love. 1John 4:7-8: "Dear friends, let us love one another, for *love comes from God.* Everyone who loves has been born of God and knows God. Whoever does not love does not know God, because God is love." That is who He is! The chapter then goes on to explain how God sent His one and only Son into the world that we might live through Him now and for eternity. And in verse 19: "We love because He first loved us." So without first knowing about God's unconditional love, I cannot even truly love on my own!

What does it look like to love as God loves? "Love is patient, love is kind. It does not envy, it does not boast, it is not proud. It is not rude, it is not self-seeking, it is not easily angered, it keeps no record of wrongs. Love does not delight in evil but rejoices with truth. It always protects, always hopes, always trusts, always perseveres." 1Corinthians 13:4-7. God's love can make our whole being complete, firm, and perfected. In God's love, there is no insecurity, no incompetency, no regrets, no worry, or no frustrations. God's love insulates us from the attacks of Satan and he has no tools to fight us when we walk in love! God's love can provide everything we need, the "joy, peace, patience, kindness, goodness, faithfulness, gentleness and self-control." Galatians 6:22: "My command is this: Love each other as I have loved you. Greater love has no one than this, that he lay down his life for his friends." John 15:12-13.

Have you ever loved someone that hated, despised, or betrayed you? If so, that is God's love flowing through you! It seems everyone is looking for this kind of love. We must start with God's love, and hold on to God's love because Satan has a convincing counterfeit; perversions of this love, to trap and deceive us. Beware!

"The Lord is close to the brokenhearted and saves those who are crushed in spirit." Psalm 34:18. Everything has been completed to heal the crushed spirit! Why are there so many crushed spirits among us? Perhaps they have not accepted God's free gift of salvation, forgiveness from the load of sin and the fullness of the Holy Spirit. Perhaps they have accepted this free gift, but are unsure it is truly free and are still struggling to please God by their good deeds or works. It may be because they do not realize God's authority and power have been given to the believer, enabling the believer to live an overcoming life. God provides this overcoming life to the believer who acts on His word, speaks to the situation to change as Jesus would do, then rises above the negative pull of Satan's bondages of sin, despair, and pain.

Well, what about those that have never heard about God? God can and will take care of them! After all, the creation, creatures, and the universe, scream that God is! His gifts of the conscience, faith, love, hope, given to us before we heard proves God is. Jeremiah 29:13 promises: "You will seek me and find me with all your heart." and Jesus says in Matthew 7:7-8: "Ask and it will be given to you, seek and you will find; knock and the door will be opened to you. For everyone who asks receives; he who seeks finds; and to him who knocks, the door will be opened." Our experiences with different cultures who have not heard of "God as we know Him" make this scripture a reality.

On one of our missionary trips to Africa, I saw God's love extended to a people that had not heard the gospel as we understand it. Our missionaries told us about reaching an isolated tribe that had previously never heard the gospel of Christ. They had no written language, no electricity, and literally no contact with the outside world. The only thing that reminded me I was in a civilized world was the occasional plane flying overhead. And yet, they adhered to a good, but different than ours, code of conduct.

They knew there was a God! They called him, "Unguy", meaning the God of the sky. Psalm 19:1 NLT says: "The heavens proclaim the glory of God. The skies display the craftsmanship." In their quest for pleasing and knowing the God of sky, they had been offering sacrifices to him for their wrong doings. When they were told the good news of Jesus they were so happy. They no longer had to sacrifice their precious goats and sheep because God had sent His son as the perfect sacrifice. "When did this happen?" they asked. Since they have no clocks nor calendars, they mark "time" by a "big rain and little rain" which occur each year. When they were told many, many "big rains" ago. Then came the profound question: "Why did you wait so long to come and tell us?" That question still rings in my ear, "Why did we wait so long?"

On a return trip to this particular tribe, the missionary asked me to preach to about twenty five of them. I considered it a privilege to be asked, but I did not know what to say. Of course all the communication was done via a precious Christian interpreter. It was time to ask for God's help! They stood in three rows outside the huts, children in front, women and then the men. All I can remember saying was what a wonderful, loving, and mighty God is, creator of all this beauty, the sky, sun, moon, stars, and all the magnificent animals and how great the gift of Jesus was for us. The rest of the service was focused on importance and power in thanksgiving, praise and just loving God.

Suddenly, all of us began singing loudly in praise and thanksgiving, but one woman was not happy at all! My interpreter moved her aside and was trying to calm her to no avail. In my ignorant bravery, I walked to the side of the hut because she indicated wildly for me to come. She put out her hands toward me and smeared fresh cow manure on my arms! They use manure to burn to cook meals and manure and mud to hold their stick huts together. I was amused, but my interpreter was not! He escorted her briskly to the back of the hut. Later, I learned what had happened. She possessed an evil spirit and the evil spirit in her did not like us praising God! The trick was on the devil, as I was not offended at all. After all, I was raised on a farm.

Now that we know, God's Spirit is available to us, be aware that there are other spirits trying to influence or even speak to us. Lying, deception, manipulation, and fear are a few of the evil spirits our enemy uses to derail our walk with God. Apostle Paul in 2 Timothy 1:7 KJV- For God has not given us a *spirit of fear;* but of power, and of love, and sound mind. Fear is sly! Life offers many opportunities for rational concerns as accidents or more recently an unhinged mass shooter in a gathering. However, we have been given power and authority over the irrational, unfounded spirit of fear. Speak to it in faith, in Jesus's name and fear has to go!

By spending time in fellowship with God and His Word, we tune our spiritual ears to hear God's message. In doing this, we automatically tune out the world and its message. Oh yes, the world's message is still heard by the natural ear, but our spiritual ear can now discern what is or is not of God. "The spirit of man (that factor in human personality which proceeds immediately from God) is the lamp of the Lord, searching all his innermost parts." Proverbs 20:27 AMP.

Get to know your spirit man. Too many rely on outward experiences or the emotions attached to the experience which is a powerful drive. These powerful emotions now hold us hostage to prolonged anger or refusal to forgive others. Prolonged anger and inability to forgive offenses have no place in our spirit. Bitterness, hostility, and hatred of others destroy our spirits, and although we may be unaware of our resentful attitude, others will not be. John 16:33: "So letting your sinful nature control your mind leads to death. But letting the Spirit control your mind leads to life and peace." Peace and life will come from God by just giving His Spirit control of our spirit! That takes trust! That takes submission to the Spirit of God!

Nicodemus, a Pharisee, slips out by night to question Jesus as to who He is and the origin of his power. Jesus replied, "I tell you the truth, unless you are born again, you cannot see the Kingdom of God."

"What do you mean?" exclaimed Nicodemus. "How can an old man go back into his mother's womb and be born again?"

Jesus replied, "I assure you no one can enter the Kingdom of God without being born of water (natural birth) and the spirit. Humans can reproduce only human life, but the Holy Spirit **gives birth to spiritual life**. So don't be surprised when I say, 'You must be born again.'" John 3:3-7 NLT.

New birth brings new life! He was preparing Nicodemus who was living under the Old Covenant of the Law for the New Covenant of God's Grace which would be unveiled after Jesus shed His blood on the cross and His resurrection.

"This is the New Covenant I will make with them after that time," says the Lord. "I will put my Laws in their hearts, and write them on their minds." Then he adds: "Their sins and lawless acts I will remember no more. And where these have been forgiven, there is no longer any sacrifice for sin." Hebrews 10:16-18. Jesus has become the guarantee of a better covenant. His shed blood on the cross paid the price required for our atonement for sin and He became our Great High Priest when we believe in Him!

1 Corinthians 2: 9-12: "No eye has seen, no ear has heard, no mind has conceived what God has prepared for those who love him. God has revealed it to us by his Spirit. The Spirit searches all things, even the deep things of God. For who among men knows the thoughts of a man except the man's spirit within him? In the same way no one knows the thoughts of God except the Spirit of God. We have not received the spirit of the world but the Spirit is from God, that we may understand what God has freely given us." The plan to restore communication from the Father's Spirit to our spirit had been accomplished!

What does God's voice sound like? John 10:27 KJV: "My sheep hear my voice, and I know them, and they follow me." It is that instant knowing - a knowing from within my core being something that I have not known beforehand. It may be words I hear in my spiritual ears directing my voice to say words that bypass my mind and come out of my mouth. Often it is a gentle rebuke, or occasionally it is a "not so gentle rebuke."

Once when we were flying in our four seater 172 Cessna, we realized we were caught in an ice storm. What should have been a 30 minute flight was now over 90 minutes. I could see ice forming on the wings, the prop was now invisible, and we were enveloped in dark grey clouds. We were lost! It felt as if we were flying straight into the ground. Pilots can easily become disoriented and confused if trusting in their own senses to determine where they are relative to the earth's surface. Even though it seems to all your senses as if it is totally wrong, pilots learn in order to survive to trust the instruments instead of their senses. There's a sermon in that somewhere.

The spirit of fear like I had never known before enveloped me. In fact, I do not think I had ever been really frightened until that day. The fear felt like ice water capturing my feet and legs and moving up my body, paralyzing the rest of me. Del was quiet; he knew he did not have the luxury to be panicked. He was flying a southern route, hoping he could find some clearing in the ice storm and to avoid crashing into nearby towers. Our young children were asleep in the back seat. And I was pleading over and over for God to help us! Not much faith, if any at all, was present in my prayers. **Faith and fear do not coexist!** That day I learned how powerful the spirit of fear can be and at that time I did not realize I could take authority over fear by commanding it to go in the name of Jesus. I was praying, pleading, silently so as not to cause my husband to panic.

When I feel my prayers are not getting answered, I have learned to ask God how I should pray. The answer came quickly. The audible voice of God from within my spirit said, *"Shut up, and pray for Del to have wisdom to land this plane!"* WOW! I would have never thought of that! I did not mind the rebuke "shut up" because I needed that to stop the cycle of fear I had allowed to circle in my mind. Instantly, overwhelming peace and comfort overflowed me melting away all fear! Thank you, God, thank you for speaking to me and for showing me how to pray. Since He said, "Land this plane," I knew we were going to land this plane instead of crashing it.

This reminded me of when Jesus told the disciples to go over to the other side of the lake in Mark 4:35-40. A fierce storm arose; they thought they were going to drown and accused Jesus of not caring! He ignored that accusation! Their fear caused them to doubt what He had commanded regarding "go to the other side." Jesus simply said, "Be still." The wind died down, the waves calmed. Waves do not behave that way: they undulate, oscillate, and fluctuate until the causative energy dies down! That impressed the disciples as they asked, "Who is this? Even the wind and the waves obey Him!"

Now the plane was still enveloped in a dense, dark cloud and we really did not know our exact location. But I had a peace that passed all understanding in my heart. Praises and thanksgiving welled up in my soul. It no longer mattered that we were lost, God knew exactly where we were. We learned by radio the Greensboro Airport and other airports in our range were already closed to traffic due to the storm. We needed a miracle. Suddenly, God graciously rolled back the clouds momentarily to show us the roof of a building. Although Del thought we were in the sand hills area, he recognized the roof of Asheboro Airport! Having flown into this airport many times, he was able to bank the plane around in the dense fog and icy rain for a near perfect landing.

When the plane had landed, Del said, "Praise the Lord!" Several men came out of the airport towards our plane. "Good, they are coming to take his pilot's license and I will not have to go through this harrowing experience ever again!" I thought to myself. Then it happened!

As men were running to our plane, they opened the door and started congratulating Del on the great job he had done in the landing! They were saying things like, "How did you do it? Several planes had to be deferred earlier and the weather is even worse now." It was then I realized what a miracle God had performed as He used Del's steady skill as a pilot. God had given him wisdom to land the plane. How good is our God!

Oh how human I am! Trusting God one moment and full of faith because God had spoken to my spirit while in the air and then totally doubting God after the landing! It reminded me of the story of Jesus and a young boy with an evil spirit. In Mark 9:22-24: the father brought his son to the disciples for healing with no results. The father asked Jesus if He could do anything, or would He take pity on us and help us. "If you can?" said Jesus. "Everything is possible for him who believes." Immediately the boy's father exclaimed, "I do believe; help me overcome my unbelief." Just as asking the Father God for direction in how to pray, we can ask Him for help in overcoming our unbelief. James 1:5 NLT: "If you need wisdom, ask our generous God and He will give it to you. He will not rebuke you for asking." We needed God's wisdom and a miracle in the storm! God's grace covered my weakness of faith that day.

As you see, one word from God to our spirit can change our whole world and that word will never contradict His written Word! When

He speaks it is profound, life changing and impacts our world for eternity. However, God has already spoken to us! We have a whole book of His words written under the influence of God's Spirit. Our enemy would like for us to remain ignorant of the Bible so he can keep us defeated, in bondage, and deceived by his ways. Our Lord provides freedom from bondage, pure joy, and a peace that passes all understanding.

Could this be why it is so difficult to commit to personal Bible study? The phone or door bell rings, children or puppies need your attention, thoughts race through your mind of things you need to do, or the reading is dull, dry. Tell your mind to be quiet, tell Satan to be quiet and find a time to devour the Word and commune with your Heavenly Father. Stay in the Word; it is our best defense against other voices that try to lead us astray. There is nothing greater than enjoying fellowship with our Father. It sets our upside down world back upright. Our perspective changes, our spirits are uplifted and communication with God becomes our passionate desire. We are already His passion!

We must be aware that there are other spirits that want to compete with God's Spirit and speak to us. Our own human spirit that is devoid of the Word of God may influence our natural thinking and we may not be aware of it. So much information comes our way, sometimes God's truth gets lost or pushed aside by the overwhelming power of what seems natural or normal. When our thinking is challenged in an area, we become uncomfortable or confrontational. We should pray, "Search me, O God and know my heart; test me and know my anxious thoughts." Psalms 139:23 NLT. Reveal to us what is in our heart or has slipped in our heart during our unawareness. Isaiah 9:16 NLT warns: "For their leaders of the people have misled them. They have led them down the path of destruction." Not only our leaders, teachers or other ideologies, but our habits and instincts are powerful influences on our thinking and behaviors.

In 2 Thessalonians 2:10 NLT: tells the plan of Satan. "He will use every kind of evil deception to fool those on their way to destruction because they refuse to love and accept the truth that would save them." Even though he is a defeated foe, he still tries to exert his influence on us. Too often, all he needs is a crack in our armor to gain entrance into our being. It may be our unwillingness to forgive, hatred, bitterness or a whole host of negative emotions we harbor in our heart. When the pressures of life are exerted, out of the abundance of the heart the mouth speaks. Satan only knows us by what we say or how we behave!

The book of Romans has a lot to say about life in the Spirit. In Chapter 1:8, Paul reveals the truth: "Therefore, there is now no condemnation for those who are in Christ Jesus, because through Christ Jesus the law of the Spirit of life set me free from the law of sin and death." The law is powerless to change the human heart. Only by accepting the perfect sin offering of Jesus's death on the cross can change the human heart! Once the heart is changed, the whole individual is changed. Once and for all the price of our sin has been paid in full!

So if you are feeling condemned, it is not from God. God gently, lovingly, convicts us to encourage us to change our ways for our own good and gives us correct solutions or answers to our problems. Satan condemns us by bringing no answers to problems, shames us, and destroys the image of ourselves. Satan tempts us with accusations like: "Just who do you think you are?" "Christians do not behave like that." "You think you are so great, if only people knew who you really are." "You are no good, or God cannot love you especially after what you have done." Satan's main goal is to shame and destroy the ones made in the image of God by attacking their minds, in an attempt to get access to their spirit! Stand on the Word of God, do not allow the enemy entrance, and be on guard as he is very cunning and deceitful. Just say, "No" to his accusations!" Remember he is the father of lies and there is no truth in him.

Remember, Jesus said, "My sheep know my voice and another they will not follow." That is where I want to be. We know Jesus would never tell us to do or be something that is contrary to the Word, but would it not be reassuring to recognize that sweet, soft voice? If we learn to recognize the voice of the Holy Spirit living within our spirit, our lives could be redirected at critical times. It may not be a warning in soft words, but an action of the Lord or His angels that stop us from making a dangerous move or mistake.

Three other students and I were driving home after our psych affiliation at 3:30 in the morning. It was 1964, no cell phones, in an old Ford Falcon and we were tired. It certainly was not wise to be on the roads at that time, but we were eager to get back to NC from Kentucky, so we left after afternoon classes. One of the students awoke and proceeded to direct me to turn on to a makeshift road in Salisbury that the neighborhood used as a shortcut. Sounds good to me! The grass and bushes were taller than my car; all I could see was the dirt path ahead of us. Suddenly, for no reason at all, my left foot jerked up and slammed on the brake, and the car choked. It was as if someone else did it! My friend then asked me why I stopped. Immediately, a train was in front of my bumper; the train's whistle started to blow, but he was already moving past my little Falcon. She said, "Man, we were lucky!" Years later, I was thinking about that incident. Luck had nothing to do with it, but God's Spirit and angel intervened! The car stopped! That is why we learn to thank Him and praise Him for the seen and unseen miracles!

It is this "spiritual person" that most of the world does not understand. It is this spiritual person that will live through all eternity. It is our spirit that we connect with God. It is this spiritual person, along with the soul, that is involved with the Near Death Experience, not the body. The death and resurrection of Jesus permitted our spirits to be born anew and to be reinstated to God as in the beginning. We are a spirit, having a human experience!

Keep Praying, Mama!

Proverbs 22:6
"Train up a child in the way he should go, and when he is old he will not turn from it."

Mr Fox:

had just transferred a patient to the step down unit when the Emergency Department called with a new admission. I was only working one to two days per week as I had young children at home. After taking the report, I knew he was a well-respected middle aged man in the community and I was secretly hoping the Lord would not lead me to him to share Jesus with him. I reasoned I might lose my job if I did! I already had a nudge from the Holy Spirit to witness to him. "But do you know who he is?" As if the Holy Spirit did not know! Sometimes He just has to laugh at us. Have you ever argued with God? How did that work out for you? Ok, I relented, I will witness to him about Jesus when he is more stable as he was gravely ill at that time.

A few hours passed before he was stable enough to talk. With great caution I approached the subject. "Mr Fox, now that you are feeling better would you like me to pray for you?" He immediately replied, "Yes, yes, PLEASE do!" Grasping my arm with such urgency, I knew this was a God moment. I do not remember what I prayed but I remember asking him, "Do you want to accept Jesus Christ into your life?"

"I really want to...but I just can't right now." was his sad reply. The Holy Spirit restrained me at this point.

Often, I surmise the person thinks he/she has committed some kind of unforgivable sin when he/she gives that kind of reply. I will tell the patient of Tex Watson's testimony that he gave several years ago while he was in prison of God's great grace and total forgiveness. On a TV program, Tex, looking at the palms of his hands said, "These hands that have the blood of 9 brutal murders on them have been washed clean with the blood of Jesus Christ." To me, that is profound because I remember the 1969 gruesome Charles Manson murders. The forgiveness of God IS profound and His grace is beyond our comprehension. However, this time I did not feel led to share Tex's testimony with Mr. Fox.

Mr. Fox continued to improve from his inferior wall myocardial infarction and was soon transferred to the step down unit. At times, he would call for me to come to his room to pray for him. Yet, he was not ready to receive Jesus. (I now think of Felix in the book of Acts waiting for a more convenient time). I do not remember exactly what I prayed but I would hear myself asking God to remove the barriers from his heart so he could receive Jesus.

Mr. Fox (3 months later):

One Friday afternoon, the Emergency Department called to give a report on a direct admission. It was Mr. Fox. By the time I hung up, he was being rolled through the door.

One glance at his grey, sallow appearance and anxious look on his face let me know his condition was severe. We helped him into the bed and I started the life saving IV. (Nurses think if they have an IV access to the body's venous system, then they can better manage any emergency.) Others were getting the oxygen started, monitor connected, and vitals signs completed. I sighed a prayer of thanks to Jesus as I saw the blood return in the IV catheter. I knew I had the IV! Also I knew his blood pressure was dropping. As I was finishing taping the IV in place, I heard the foreboding "agonal" sound. (When death occurs, residual air in the lungs escapes making a certain, unforgettable sound.) He was gone!

The Monitor pattern was now ventricular fibrillation. The heart is no longer pumping blood, but erratic electrical waves are present on the monitor. Immediately I started compressions, asked for the defibrillator, and someone to do manual ventilation and to push IV medications. The full code was just getting started when I heard myself say, "God, don't let him die, he "ain't" ready!" It just came up from my innermost being. The first time I heard that statement was when it came out of my mouth. My next thought was, "You said "*ain't*" to God!" Wow, "*ain't*" to God?

Seconds later, I saw Mr. Fox move his leg. The monitor pattern was somewhat normal even though he had not been defibrillated (shocked)! He soon began breathing on his own and had a pulse. He was alive! He was alive just before we had a chance to defibrillate him.

The cardiac arrest and treatment left him temporarily drowsy. Later, I was administering some medication through the IV, he opens his eyes, and said, "Thank you, thank you so much."

"Yes, you really gave me a scare, but I just kept praying for you," I responded.

"I know and keep praying for me, please."

He indicated he was now ready to receive Jesus! Again I do not remember exactly what I prayed but I included the simple prayer of asking Jesus to come into his life and heart, so he could forgive others and accept Jesus's forgiveness of his sin. I do remember thanking God for sparing his life and for His marvelous grace.

In talking with Mr. Fox, he did not have a home church nor anyone to mentor him. A pastor I knew was willing to visit him in the hospital. Later, he joined the pastor's church and he was a faithful member of that church for several years.

Mr. Fox (3 weeks after the cardiac arrest):

I was at home one morning, and our phone rang. I answered it cautiously as we had been getting prank calls. A voice was moaning, possibly crying so I said, "Say something or I'll have to hang up!"

"No please don't, this is Mr. Fox. Do you remember me?"

"Of course, I do! How are you?" I responded.

After a long pause, he said "I had to call you and thank you for what you did for me that evening.""

"Oh that's what we do for everyone"... He cut me off in mid-sentence.

"No, I mean for holding my hand! If you had turned me loose I would be in hell today!"

Now, he had my full attention! He continued, "I was being forcefully pulled down a black, cold tunnel, so cold and black the blackness went completely through me. It was totally frightening. Then I stopped at a gate and something or someone was just about to push me through when you pulled me back up the tunnel."

"Ok, ok" my mind was spinning, what could I say? I think I said something about believing him and how great our God is to spare his life. It is important for patients that have a Near Death Experience to be believed.

He then told me why he felt he could not accept Jesus earlier. It was so deeply personal to him and he was not willing to let it go until that frightening experience of facing death at the gates of hell. As we know, God's forgiveness is greater than any weight we may attach to any sin or secret sin!

Some time later, I learned his mother was a praying woman and prayed for him daily. I had always wondered why I said *"ain't"* to God. I remembered elementary teachers in the 50's correcting us when we would inadvertently let "ain't" slip. I know that statement did not originate in my brain but it seemed to come up from within my spirit.

Many years later, a friend of mine gave me a possible answer. She said that could have been his mother's prayers still at work on this earth long after her death! I can just hear that mother praying, "Lord, don't let my boy die, he "ain't" ready!" It was her faithful prayers at work in this atmosphere of this world that were holding him to the earth's realm! It certainly was not my hand that pulled him back from the gates of hell. I was too busy doing external compressions on his chest.

We serve an awesome God! Words are powerful and alive. When a word is spoken in prayer, it remains active in the spiritual realm, no time limit. Remember this while praying for others who need God in their life. I have been praying for a famous lady, unknown to me except by TV, for over forty five years to come to know Jesus as her Lord and Savior. It was in 1972, I was angry and complaining about her to the Lord, asking Him to change her attitude. I heard inside of me the Lord say, "Why don't you stop complaining and start praying for her to know me!" Wow! Occasionally, I would sense she is close to changing, but her behavior and words tell me she has not committed her life to the Lord. In Matthew 7:20: Jesus says, "Thus, by their fruit you will recognize them." No judgement needed, I am just observing the fruit, and praying! I will allow God to do the real judging.

What a blessing it is to intercede in prayer for someone God deems worthy of salvation that you may not know. It may not materialize in your lifetime as it did for Mr. Fox's mother, but it will come to pass. I challenge you to try this. Ask God who He would like for you to intercede for in prayer. There are plenty on God's list, I am sure. Then enjoy the challenge!

Keep praying for your loved ones, too! Declare that your loved ones, children, and grandchildren will know, serve, and love the Lord with all their hearts. Declare that they may teach their children to do so, also.

Isaiah 54:13: "All your sons will be taught by the Lord, and great will be your children's peace."

Mr. Fox (7 years later):

The first time I shared Mr. Fox's experience publicly was in our Sunday school class one

Sunday. I had only shared with a few friends before that Sunday. When I went to work that afternoon, I learned Mr. Fox had another cardiac arrest at home. All the paramedics could do was reestablish a heart rhythm. He was declared brain dead and was on life support. While the electroencephalogram (EEG) showed no brain waves, I knew his spirit was more than alive with Jesus! Our spirits do not register on an EEG; they are too highly developed to do that!

At that time, I was only working one or two days a week and hardly ever worked on Sunday. Could it be that God orchestrated that day so I could say goodbye to Mr. Fox? I like to think so. I stood by his bedside and thanked the Lord for the work He had done in Mr. Fox's life, all praises to our Lord.

I had not met his family before that day. His wife had requested an update on his condition. When I opened the door, she looked astonished to see me and said, "You are the one he talked about!" I suppose he had told her about the experience, but how did she know it was me? Sometimes two people are connected by an experience even if unknown to each other.

The plan was to repeat the EEG in the AM and discontinue the life support if there was still no brain activity. I always encourage the family to talk to the patient just in case he/she can hear. Later, the family may be comforted by what he/she said to his/her loved one. The wife and friend said their goodbyes once again and left to get dinner. Shortly after they left, his heart rate gradually slowed and then ceased. He was gone again, but this time he was in heaven.

Malachi 3:11: "And I will rebuke the devourer for your sakes, and he shall not destroy the fruits of your ground; neither shall your vine cast her fruit before the time in the field, saith the LORD of hosts."

Speak to It!

I Corinthians 15:42:
"*The body that is sown is perishable, it is raised imperishable; it is sown in dishonor, it is raised in glory; it is sown in weakness, it is raised in power; it is sown a natural body; it is raised a spiritual body.*"

Luke 9:1:
When Jesus had called the Twelve together, He gave them power and authority to drive out all demons and to cure all diseases. So we have been given the power and authority but how do we do it?

In Mark chapter 11: We are told about Jesus and His disciples leaving Bethany for Jerusalem. Being hungry, they saw a fig tree in the distance but the closer they came to it they saw it had no figs but only leaves because it was not the season for figs (The fig tree represents Israel)! Verse 12: Then he said to the tree, "May no one ever eat fruit from you again." And His disciples heard Him say it. (Israel's season was defiance, they were not ready to receive Jesus and His Kingdom as was evident by the leaders' attitude towards His ministry. Seventy years later, the temple was destroyed by the Romans). Jesus continued on His mission that day, cleansing the temple of those who were buying and selling in the temple courts.

Mark 11:20: In the morning, as they went along, they saw the fig tree withered from the roots. Peter remembered what Jesus had said to the tree so he said, "Rabbi, look! The fig tree you cursed has withered!"

Verse 22-25: "Have faith in God," Jesus answered. "I tell you the truth, if anyone says to this mountain, 'Go, throw yourself into the sea,' and does not doubt in his heart but believes that what he **says** will happen, it will be done for him. Therefore I tell you, whatever you ask for in prayer, believe that you have received it, and it will be yours. And when you stand praying, if you hold anything against anyone, forgive him, so that your Father in heaven may forgive you your sins."

Forgive, believe, pray, and **speak** to the things we want to change! Words are creative and powerful once stated. Speak to the mountains of fears, anxieties, hurts, diseases, despair, offenses, pain, and lack in our lives to leave. Declare that peace, tranquility, forgiveness, faith, joy, health, and for your needs to be met. Too often it is easier to *speak about* the problem rather than to *speak to* the problem.

Ms. Kitty

Ms. Kitty was a sweet but spicy, frail elderly lady who prided herself on being able to live independently despite her many chronic conditions. She had compromised lung condition, diabetes, high blood pressure, and end stage heart failure. Now, she had a dissecting aortic aneurysm just above the renal arteries. Surgery was not an option for her, nor did she want surgery. She said softly, "I really would like to see my grandson, Kyle."

He was her closest living relative and was flying in the next day.

Suddenly, I heard myself say, "Well, don't die till you see him." It just came up from somewhere in my innermost being.

"Can I do that?" she said cautiously.

"Yes you can!" I heard myself say! What did I just say? How can you deliver on that promise! How quickly the accusing voice of doubt comes to make you question your stand in faith. When doubt comes, refocus on the truth. I could not have delivered on that promise, only God could! Realizing this, I prayed for her and asked the Lord to grant her desire. I will admit it was with shaky faith that I prayed because the war was raging inside about what I had promised her. Her feet and lower legs were already cyanotic, pedal pulses were long gone and her kidneys were showing diminished functioning. It was amazing that she was lucid at all since her blood chemistries were so eschewed due to kidney failure.

The next day when I returned, the curtain was pulled! After a patient dies, we pull the curtain out of respect for them. My heart sank! But in the report I learned she had requested the curtain be pulled to give Kyle and her some privacy! Whew! She was alert and aware throughout the next day, also. God is so good. She asked for one day; He gave her two! The next morning her condition was definitely worse. She opened her eyes briefly when she saw me. Softly she said, "I am ready to die. Can I do that?"

"Yes, you can," I said quietly.

"Ok, I will," she said matter of factly. "I want to say goodbye to Kyle." This time she had a peaceful, contented look on her face as we prayed, thanking Jesus for what He had done in her life. So often a patient is ready and wanting to die, but they need permission from their loved ones to do so. Why are we so hesitant to grant them this last request? Perhaps it is our own hesitancy to face death ourselves.

Just think about it! How powerful are our words, both for the positive as well as the negative force in our life. Kyle stayed at her bedside until she was ushered into the Kingdom of Heaven later that morning. What a way to go!

Psalms 116:15.
"Precious in the sight of the Lord is the death of his saints."

Psalms 117: 2:
"For great is his love toward us, and the faithfulness of the Lord endures forever."

II Thessalonians 3:5:
"May the Lord direct your hearts into God's love and Christ's perseverance."

The Soul

---

3 John 1:2:
"Beloved, I pray that you may in all things prosper and be in health, just as your soul prospers."

Psalms 103:1-3 KJV:
"-Bless the Lord, O my soul: and all that is within me, bless his his holy name. Bless the Lord, O my soul, and forget not all His benefits: Who forgiveth thee all thine iniquities; and healeth all thy diseases."

If we connect with God through our spiritual realm, we connect with our environment through our soul.

What is the soul? The soul is composed of the mind, the will, and the emotions. When the soul, (mind, will, emotions) worship God, it is easy for the body and spirit to enter in the praises. It is a powerful act when all the whole person, spirit, soul, and body enters into the unified act of worship by praise to the Heavenly Father. Tears in eyes, smile on the face, uplifted hands, dancing feet, and vocal cords begin singing praises, and the whole person begins to worship his Creator with explicit joy and adoration.

A demonstration of a soul's behavior is easily seen in children. Unfortunately, they are learning the skills of deception or manipulation to achieve their selfish goals. They do not have to be taught to be selfish-it comes naturally. "It is mine!" Their first response when their toy is threatened, even though their hands are full of toys. When they do something wrong, most of the time they will try to hide it. If caught, the answer is, "It was not my fault. He/she made me do it." That behavior may seem cute or not worthy of correction as we remember our own childish behavior. However, if unaddressed it may give the enemy a foothold in the child's life. We as parents have to teach them to assume responsibility, confront the lying, manipulation, and teach them how to respect others and themselves. No small task, to be sure!

A lie distorts reality until the lie becomes the "truth" to the deceived. Loss of reality is the beginning of insanity. In other areas of our life whether it is immoral behaviors, stealing, cursing, being envious or jealous of others and even murder result from the searing of the conscience and loss of reality. Excuses and blaming others will soothe for a while and may become the artificial "truth", but the ache inside our spirit will eventually result in the breakdown in the spirit, then the soul and body. Repressed anger, guilt, shame, and insecurity have a way of escaping through fractures in our soul. A healthy soul must be cleansed of these negative mindsets and emotions to function in a healthy manner. A simple solution to this problem is the soul must die to this world's ways. Simple, but yet it is complicated. Because we are so human, we fall back into wrongdoing; we are creatures of habit, and truthfully, we have a carnal nature. Dying to this nature takes an ongoing, vigilant awareness of sin and our willingness to repent.

Just exactly what is sin, iniquity, and transgression? According to an online article, sin, iniquity, and transgression are defined by the Hebrew interpretations. "*Chattah*, is translated as sin, means to miss the mark. *Awon* is translated as iniquity, relates more to inner character and points to an intentional twisting of a given standard. *Pesha*, often translated as transgression is more willful rebellion (Phillips *The Mystery*). "Transgression is knowing where the line is, but trespassing on purpose. Iniquity is wicked, corrupt, premeditated evil; and if allowed to continue it leads to a reprobate mind with no fear of God. Iniquity can be forgiven if it is recognized as evil; confession is made; repentance is declared; and forgiveness is received from God. Sin is doing wrong against God or against our fellow man. It may be knowing to do what is right and neglecting or refusing to do it. Pride always leads to sin. All these sins need to be acknowledged, forgiveness sought, repentance established, and then one must choose to live in humility to God and others.

All three topics are mentioned in the two verses of Psalms 51:1-2: "Have mercy on me, O God, according to your unfailing love; according to your great compassion blot out my transgression. Wash away all my iniquity and cleanse me from my sin." King David had committed adultery with Bathsheba; this sin resulted in pregnancy. To cover the sin, he called her husband home from the battlefield so he could spend the night with his wife. Her husband, Uriah the Hittite, was an honorable man. After eating and drinking with King David for two days, David tried to get him drunk. Uriah still would not go home to his wife. He felt it would not be appropriate for him to enjoy being home when the other soldiers were still on the battlefield. King David wrote a letter to the general, Joab, telling him to place Uriah at the front of a furious battle, withdrawing from him, so he would be killed. This was a premeditated murder. King David thought he had covered his sin, but Nathan, the prophet, confronted the King with his sin and iniquity. As a result of this iniquity, the child died and calamity struck King David's household. The fallout of iniquity often involves others who may be totally innocent.

Some believe in a generational sin of iniquity which can be passed on by our forefathers. Is it the iniquity, or is it the strong influence the iniquity has on our souls? If the iniquity is excused and made acceptable by the parent, the child may have difficulty in knowing the truth and to distinguish between right from wrong. The individual may not be aware of the influence, but may wonder why he/she cannot obtain victory over certain sins. Hebrews 12:1 NLT: "Therefore, since we are surrounded by such a huge cloud of witness to the life of faith, let us strip off every weight that slows us down, especially the sin that so easily trips us up. And let us run with endurance the race God has set before us." When Jesus came, He ushered in a new covenant. Hebrews 10:16: "This is the covenant I will make with them after that time, says the Lord. I will put my laws in their hearts, and I will write them on their minds." Then he adds: "Their sins and lawless acts I will remember no more." Ask the Lord to reveal any hidden sins; seek forgiveness and forgive our forefathers so that no root of bitterness may grow.

In the Old Testament, one can easily see the influence of the father's sin replaying in the son's life. The history of the Kings tells of the many times the sons did what was evil in the Lord's sight, just as their fathers. There were exceptions like young Joash whose life was spared from evil Queen Athaliah when she killed the other princes. Joash remained hidden in the temple until at age of seven when he was crowned King. Joash did what was right in the eyes of the Lord. Godly teaching does make a difference.

Yes, our spirit man is born again when we repent, but the soul needs to be constantly guarded as it is constantly subjected to the ways of the world. A lot of God's grace is needed here. A constant realization of who we are in Christ Jesus, the payment He made for our sins through the cross and His resurrection, provides the answer for our souls. Our love for the Father compels us to live a "Christ centered" life. That is what Jesus was talking about... "that they may have life, and have it to the full" (John 10:10b). There is no room for the world's ways when we are full of Jesus!

It is interesting how we succumb to the lies of Satan if the sway of the multitude uses their rational means to trap us. After all, the educated, powerful, or respectable are supposed to be leading us. Right? While listening to a documentary on vaping and the history of smoking, the youth in attendance were horrified that the medical profession was promoting smoking in the 1950's as a healthy endeavor. My dad was not about to buy it! His argument with that idea was that all the chemicals put on the plants along with the tars in tobacco should not be introduced into the body's fragile lung tissue.

Now, our youth have been educated to the dangers of smoking, but they were using that to support their argument for vaping, saying it was safe because that is what was being presented to them. They were not convinced when the narrator was warning them of the detrimental effects of nicotine and other agents from vaping on the lungs, heart, and other organs. This documentary was made before the deaths from vaping had occurred. It is wise to question the validity of new concepts and who is making a monetary profit.

My heart aches for the many women and men that have been snared and manipulated by the abortion industry's half-truths and outright lies. For these dear ones, I have hope for you if you endured an abortion. God's grace is available especially for you! If you have not already done so, just ask Father God for forgiveness that is made possible by Jesus's sacrifice on the cross. Accept Jesus into your life; accept your forgiveness; remind yourself of your forgiveness every time Satan tries to make you doubt it. Do not allow Satan to steal anymore of your peace; just trust Jesus to set you free and completely make you whole once more. Many women and men have been set free through the power of Jesus's love and forgiveness. And know this, you will see that child again in Heaven! All is not lost if you make plans to go to Heaven.

This evil plan of abortion was being devised many years before January 22,1973 when the Supreme Court ruled abortion to be legal. Margaret Sanger (1879-1966), a leader of this ideology, is credited with founding Planned Parenthood in 1942. Sanger promoted the idea of eugenics; the belief the human population could be improved by controlled breeding. Undesirable traits, mental disorders, certain races, and diseases (for which we now have cures), should not be allowed to reproduce (Brown, *Margaret)*. Is this the thinking that led to Hitler's attempt to have a Supreme Race? The deception increased in the 1960's: we were being told that abortion was more humane than allowing an unwanted child to be born into poverty or later being a victim of physical abuse. But abortion seems to have increased child abuse crimes. Abortion lowers the value of the child's life! We were told it would stop women's death due to abortions being done outside medical clinics. This is not always true either. Pregnancy due to rape and incest pose difficult questions for which our Father can supply the answers. I know an absolutely beautiful lady that was a product of a violent rape. The truth is, abortions have always been legal in cases to preserve the mother's life, which are rare, and when the child is no longer viable.

Abortion did not become real to me until about 1974 when my nursing students were asked to observe a saline injection. Standing there, I knew the hypertonic saline injected into the uterus was going to suck out the fluid within the baby's body. Infant's fluid content is 80% of their body's weight. It was so surreal, death within a sterile environment! As I stood watching, I distinctly heard the voice of God say, "You are party to murder!" I knew it was God because that is not my language style. My lackadaisical attitude toward abortion was changed forever. The students and I left the room under a cloud of somberness as if the procedure had not happened. Sometime later, a physician was discussing with me the kinds of available birth control to use after the birth of our last child. He stated, "Not to worry, if you do get pregnant, we will take care of it." Suddenly, I heard within myself, "No! you will not kill my baby!" The soul suffers when we fall prey to the lies we are led to believe, especially by professionals that should be our leaders. The power of deception still astonishes me, all the more as I age.

Even King David seemed to step outside of himself as he talked to his soul demanding his soul to obey the Word and praise our Lord. One of King David's greatest accomplishments was his purity and consistency in offering thanksgiving and praises to our Lord. His trust and love for God compelled him to praise God when things were good; when circumstances were against him or when he did not feel like it, his praise continued. David's praise grew out of a sincere heart of thanksgiving. In fact we are instructed in Psalms 100:4 KJV- "Enter into his gates with thanksgiving, and into his courts with praise: be thankful unto him, and bless his name." David tells us to first be thankful and then praises will well up within our hearts for God.

Although it is our born again spirit that makes praise and thanksgiving possible, it is with our soul that we demonstrate our thankfulness, worship, and praise to our Lord. We lay aside our selfishness, egotism, and self-absorbed living and focus on our Heavenly Father and His attributes. We are totally consumed by His abounding love for us, His astounding forgiveness for our failures, His unsurpassable faithfulness to us. Thus, our hearts now are able to humbly thank the Lord for just who He is and praises begin to well up within our souls. This form of praise is pure in motive. There is no asking for anything, just praise and adoration to our Lord, just for who He is and loving Him for being our God. It is here we can dwell in the secret places of our Lord! It is here He speaks to us, and our souls are refreshed and strengthened to meet the demands and trials of life.

Under the leadership of our Heavenly Father, our souls have the capability to be molded into an honorable being. It all depends on how we allow Him to develop our minds, use our will to choose wisely, and to control our emotions! This is a beautifully integrated system that flows in its operation of joy, peace, and contentment. Simply put, all our cares are placed upon Him, all our trust is in His plan for us, and all our faith in His promises now become operational. Such freedom to know our Heavenly Father is in control of our lives. That is an abundant life!

The Mind

Proverbs 14:15
"A simple man believes anything, but a prudent man gives thought to his steps."

What is the mind, the brain? The brain executes 100 trillion connections and 100 billion neurons to interpret information within the body and in the outside world. The brain with spinal cord are responsible for intelligence, memory, creativity, imaginations, emotions, thoughts, balance, communication, and the movement of arms and legs. It processes information from the five senses, interprets pain, and generates a plethora of hormones and neurotransmitters to activate the autonomic nervous system. The three main areas are the cerebrum, cerebellum, and the brain stem. The frontal lobe is for social interactions, personality expression, and attention holding; the parietal lobe functions as an interpreter for the senses; the temporal lobe is for hearing, language, and memory; occipital lobe is for interpretation of visual stimuli. This magnificent three pound organ uses 20% of our energy although it is only 3% of body mass on the average (NINDS *Brain Basics*).

We have many levels of intellectual abilities and are able to do many great things with this intelligence. The greater "Intelligence Designer" had trillions and trillions of templates available to Him to make so many people so different, and yet similar! Not only in differences in appearance but in thinking, reacting, and emotional responses. That is His finger print seen on all creation! And He has enough finger prints to give each of us our own copy after a few weeks of gestation, even if you are an identical twin! What a mighty God!

If the brain is the processor of information, could it be instrumental in relaying this information to the mind? Or is the mind relaying the information to the brain? How do our thoughts develop? Some say thoughts just appear! How can that be? A thought is a reactionary or learned response to pleasant or not so pleasant situations previously experienced. How we react to situations takes thinking and that requires discipline! So the mind is in collaboration with the brain, but seems to possess greater abilities than the brain.

The story of the rich man and the poor beggar Lazarus in Luke 16:19-31- gives us some insight into the thinking after death. After a miserable life of suffering, Lazarus died. The rich man died later, ended up in torment, and saw Lazarus in paradise with Abraham. He asked Abraham to let Lazarus bring him a drop of water to cool his parched tongue. Later, he asked if someone could be sent to warn his five brothers not to come to this place. Now we know the rich man's body was in the grave and his brain was already decomposed. Yet he could see, remember, communicate, think, hear, reason, feel pain and thirst. Back to our question, the brain and mind cannot be the same.

The brain and its functions are part of this earthly realm as is demonstrated by certain biological tests that can be performed. The mind is full of wisdom, intelligence, emotions, compassion, and love as is evidenced by the rich man's statements. So we must have a soul with a mind of its own that moves with our spirit from this state to the next when we die. Is this part of our personality? Is this how we will be known in eternity? Is that how we can know things intuitively while here on earth? Is this why certain neurodegenerative diseases or brain trauma steal the individual's ability to function but they still retain some of their personality? The mind is more intelligent and wise than the brain because it knows all the brain knows and much more. While the brain is part of the physical body and is subject to death, the mind seems to be a part of our eternal soul.

According to most neuroscientists, there are three to seven or more levels of consciousnesses in the brain. To be conscious is to be aware of oneself, the surroundings, the date and time. I always assessed my patients as being "alert and aware" but what did that mean?

This phenomena of knowing the thought processes of another is purely subjective. All I could tell is, if they were acting or responding appropriately to their surroundings according to me! Case in point, once I asked a young teen if he would cough for me after waking up from general anesthesia. He stared at me a few seconds and said, "But I don't need to cough." That made perfect sense to him. Why would you cough unless you felt the need to do so? He did not understand I was trying to evaluate his ability to manage his own airway after general anesthesia to prevent choking or aspiration by coughing.

Consciousness is the ability to feel and experience who we are and starts to develop in infancy. This conscious state allows us to think, make decisions, declare our will, to have desires for or have aversions against things. The conscious state is commander in chief and the other levels of consciousness take orders from it. This conscious state has input from our 5 senses, to hear, see, smell, touch and taste (Wilken, *Freud's Model*). These senses help lead and guide our actions and thoughts. While imagination does begin consciously, it does so without any sensory input from the five senses! Just imagine that.

The conscious state is only 10-15% of the brain's functioning. However, it is the commander in chief of motor function as well as our emotions and response to our environment (Wilken, *Freud's Model).* So we **can** control our emotions, positive or negative, by our thoughts and words! Our behaviors, actions and reactions can be controlled with enough determination, desire, practice, and discipline over time. We must take charge of our thoughts in order to be in charge of our words, behaviors, and actions.

Most agree it takes 21 days to break a bad habit, 21 days to substitute a good habit for a bad habit and I believe another 21 days to seal the deal (*Habit Formation).* I have not been able to do this without the help of the Heavenly Father. This is a vigilante process to hold the gain! "For as he thinks in his heart, so is he." Proverbs 23:7: "Keep and guard your heart with all vigilance and above all that you guard, for out of it flows the springs of life." Proverbs 4:23 Amplified.

The subconscious mind is thousands times more powerful than the conscious mind and is 50-60% of the brain's capacity. It's always on duty. It automatically controls breathing, heart contractions, digestion, circulation and is on duty day and night. It is a dormant storage bank for memories and experiences both good or bad that may be pull up by the conscious mind. Thus, it affects behavior, thoughts, feelings, and all kinds of actions because it obediently delivers on what the conscious mind demands (Wilken, *Freud's Model*).

Therefore, if we choose to dwell on the negative, the subconscious pulls up all the negative emotions associated with that thought or experience. Conversely, if we choose to dwell on positive thoughts and actions, the subconscious pulls up all positive emotions associated with that action or thought. Try it! Think of a past experience like Christmas. Positive feelings like love, joy and acceptance if it was a good experience or negative feelings like bitterness, hurt and loneliness if it was a bad experience. These emotions automatically come into our minds with little effort on our part. So we must choose to think on the positive instead of negative and keep our subconscious mind free of negative thoughts as much as possible.

Deep seated beliefs, faith in God, loyalty, justice, and love make up the foundation of the positive subconscious mind. Memorizing scriptures is an excellent method of protecting your positive subconscious. The negative mindset harbors fear, anxiety, hate, worry, insecurity, envy, and jealousy. You get to choose! For most of us, a negative mindset just comes naturally; a positive mindset requires us to change one's thoughts, refusing the negative and declaring what is positive.

Pay attention to what you hear! It is interesting that our Creator did not give us a mechanism of stopping what we hear! We can close our mouths and stop saying words if we choose to do it. We can close our eyes if we choose not to see. But we cannot choose what we hear. Therefore, diligence must be taken when negative, untrue words are being said about other groups of people. Prejudices develop when these attitudes and opinions based on untruths, partial truths are accepted as the truths. Negative words, such as gossip, pollute our minds and memories causing us to develop negative attitudes toward others. This should not be! It is dangerous to be present at a juicy gossip session as you may be blamed for the gossip, speaking from experience! Walk away if possible, ask if you can have the person in question to verify the information, or reveal the truth if you know it. Satan is behind these lies and uses lies to destroy people and their lives both in prejudices and gossiping. Be aware of the truth only and pray for cleansing of the subconscious mind and memory. This is one way to beat Satan at his game.

Sleep is thought to happen in the subconscious even though we are unconscious of surroundings during sleep. But the sleep state can be aroused unlike in the unconscious state. Perhaps sleep has a level of its own. We know that sleep can be interrupted by alarms, barking dogs, pain, or tactile stimulation.

Good quality sleep and its health benefits have been known for a long time. Until sleep studies (polysomnography) were available, we did not have a good way of evaluating sleep. The sleep brain waves as they occur during a sleep episode indicate the level of the brain's activity during sleep. REM, rapid eye movement, is thought to be the deepest level of sleep and occurs at different intervals during sleep. During REM sleep, the brain waves perk up, the waves somewhat resemble its awakened state, and our muscles are temporarily paralyzed. Some people report being awakened during this brief state and are unable to move. Weird feeling, I know (*Sleep Cycle*).

Sleep repairs the body, reboots the immune system, and promotes healing by ridding it of debris. Restful sleep promotes many positive effects on the musculoskeletal system, heart, and circulatory system, oxygen consumption, as well as mental acuity. Restless leg syndrome, narcolepsy, insomnia, sleep walking, and talking are some disorders revealed in sleep studies. Chronic obstructive sleep apnea (severe snoring with periods of apnea) produces detrimental effects on the body's ability to function due to lack of oxygen to vital organs (*Sleep Cycle*).

How beautifully and wonderfully our Creator designed us!

Another phenomena of sleep is sleepwalking and talking. It is thought to occur during deep REM sleep. Sleepwalking and talking is done with no alertness or remembrance. I've been accused by my husband and my parents of doing these activities in the past.

On one occasion, my husband told our friends that I had performed CPR on him during sleep. Everyone laughed; I denied it. Two weeks later, I was in the ICU, the patient in bed #2 had a cardiac arrest and I started CPR. I even called out for the defibrillator! Then the patient kicked me! Since he showed this sign of life, I looked up to see his monitor pattern. What I saw was the clipper ship hanging on the wall above our bed! "What is that doing in ICU?" was my first thought. Suddenly, I realized I was at home. I had been doing chest compressions on my husband's side again in my sleep! My heart was racing; Now, I was really awake! I breathed quietly, moved slowly out of my CPR position so as not to awaken him and tried to calm down my excitement. Imagine that! If CPR compressions did not awaken him, what could? But the dream had been so very real, complete with emotions, in technicolor and panorama vision!

Care should be taken as to what we let into our subconscious minds. Pre-knowledge, memories, intuition, and daydreaming can be found in the subconscious. Hypnosis is believed to happen here. God has given us control of our mind by the decisions and choices we make. Why would I relinquish that beautiful, precious gift to someone else? Plus, totally emptying our minds during hypnosis or any other activity is an invitation for our enemy to play havoc with our mind. Be aware, our enemy is always looking for a way to deceive us.

The unconsciousness level is 30-40% of the brain's capacity (Wilken, *Freud Model)*. Coma is a classical example of unconsciousness when there is no purposeful movement, unable to arouse, and no response to stimuli. The unconscious may have some automatic reflexes as vision, breathing, yawning, heart beating, hearing, or digestion. To be truly unconscious there is no responsiveness even to painful stimuli. Thus, it is assumed that pain cannot be felt during the unconscious state. This, I do not know as I am conscious!

Fainting or syncope is a temporary loss of consciousness for a short duration when the BP drops, thus impeding blood flow to the brain. A few causes of fainting are emotional stresses such as fear and anxiety, or due to intense physical pain, heart arrhythmia, standing too long in one position, and being in a poorly ventilated, crowded room. Dehydration or needing to eat along with certain medications may be the contributing factor. Remove the causative factor, position the person flat to facilitate good blood flow to the brain and thus the return of consciousness. Fainting in a healthy individual is usually not serious but it should be followed up by a physician.

Altered level of consciousness is usually due to some type of sedative, hypnotic, or hallucinate drug being taken. The different degrees of consciousness depends on the amount of drug or the individual's response to the drug. Even if the dose is the same, age and weight the same, each person may respond differently to the drug. Unfortunately, accidental overdoses occur in this manner. Therefore, self-medication is a very dangerous activity because no one knows how his/her body may react to the drug or dose. It is not a one size fits all!

Moderate sedation medication is given in a controlled, well monitored, environment by physicians and nurses for certain procedures for sedation and pain control. The airway must be independently maintained by the patient so as not to slip into unconsciousness as during general anesthesia and cease to breathe. Under these drugs, the patient will answer questions correctly, state who they are, carry on conversation and seem to be alert and aware. However, they will have no recollection of anything they said or the happenings during the procedure that was performed. Total amnesia with the individual seemingly totally awake: scary, is it not? I always pray for the Lord to protect my mind from evil when my mind is subjected to these medications when I am not in control.

I remember when these classes of drugs came into being. My concern was the ill effects when the drug hit the streets. One anesthesiologist said, "Don't worry about that. They will not be able to remember where they bought it so they can not go back for more." That was comical, but I know human nature. Sometime later, I started hearing about a "date rape drug." This illegal form of the drug is given to an unsuspecting person, who will do and act whatever way the perpetrators dictate, with no memory of the action, while seemingly alert! The drug had hit the streets.

Another level of consciousness which is gaining attention is the super consciousness. This is a level of consciousness that is thought to be above one's own self-awareness. New Age, yoga, reincarnation, spirit guides, and similar belief systems subscribe to super consciousness. Some even believe in the powers of psychic spirits and karma. This move in spiritualism is alarming as it shows our desire to be enlightened without the guidance of God. This is the mindset of Eve which caused the fall in the Garden of Eden. Satan tells Eve, "When you eat of it your eyes will be opened, and you will be like God, knowing good from evil." Genesis 3:5b. That sounded harmless to them, also.

Reincarnation is gaining ground and is another mind game. The truth is found in

Hebrews 9:27a: "Just as man is destined to die once, and after that to face judgement, so Christ was sacrificed once to take away the sins of many people." The Bible, the truth, warns us and does not condone such actions and beliefs. So, just what are these paranormal experiences? Could they be from the "familiar spirits" that we are warned about in the Bible?

If our Heavenly Father does not direct our spirit and soul at this super conscious level, we are easy prey for our enemy to confuse or deceive us. Satan always distorts God's Word to deceive us. "Be sober, be vigilant; because your adversary the devil, as a roaring lion, walketh about, seeking whom he may devour." 1 Peter 5:8 KJV.

Please note: the devil is not a lion and if he were a roaring lion, he should not be feared. We learned in the Bush of Africa how lions hunt. The old toothless or lazy male lions are positioned to roar on one side of the prey. Then they let out a ferocious roar! The prey anxiously run away from the roar, right into the mouths of the waiting killer females on the opposite side! One morning, our guide backed our open topped vehicle between two sleeping male lions, about five feet away. One of the Maasai guides threw snack boxes and even punched them with a stick! Finally, one lion raised his sleepy head with a freshly blood stained mane, and looked at us, then went back to sleep! I could not believe what I was seeing! What the guide knew was the lions were full from the night's hunt and were no danger to us. My limited thinking did not have access to the knowledge of an experienced native!

Often we think the brain is mostly responsible for knowledge. However, to quote Albert Einstein, "Imagination is more important than knowledge. Knowledge is limited. Imagination circles the world (Einstein, *Quotes*)!" Children start imaginary play at 18-24 months. Teens, and adults are frequently daydreaming; we adults call it "thinking outside the box." Imagination is a powerful force producing images, scenes and sensations in the brain without any input of the five senses! These images can be objects, people, events or happenings that never existed now, or ever in the past. There is no reality to the imagination!

Reality and imagination flow in opposite directions in the brain. Real events from the eyes flow up to the brain's occipital lobe (visional center) to the parietal lobe for interpretation. But imagined images originate in the parietal lobe, flow in the opposite direction down from parietal to the occipital lobe! Thus, it is imagined, not information from the five senses, but the mind builds the scene out of nothing (Porter, *The Neuroscience of Imagination*). Imagination serves in problem solving, preserving memory, developing theories, inventions, and it also piques our curiosity.

Creativity is doing something meaningful with what has been imagined. It is termed "creative" but actually we do not create anything. Ecclesiastes 1:9: "There is nothing new under the sun" to quote a very wise man. We've just simply imagined how to invent something out of the available, known or unknown, resources. Radio waves, electricity, ultra-violent rays, X-rays, smart phones, television and now quantum physics are some of man's creative inventions, imagined first, then created from the resources that have always been available.

So, why did our Creator include something so elusive as imagination in our design? Was our imagination in the original design to connect us to God for communication? Is this how Adam and Eve were able to commune so freely each day with Him before the fall? This "God's sense" or **faith** enables us to see, hear, and know what cannot be sensed in the natural world with our five natural senses. We are encouraged to walk by faith and not by sight, to hear the voice of God, and to know beyond our knowing the things of God which we call prophecy. There is so much knowledge in the Spiritual realm that we do not currently know. The Apostle Paul was talking about this in 1 Corinthians 13:12: KJV: "For we see through a glass, darkly; but then face to face: now I know in part; but then shall I know even as also I am known." In Hebrews 11:3: " By faith we understand that the universe was formed at God's command, *so that what is seen was not made out of what was visible."* There is so much more than this visible realm.

Could it be we needed an avenue to connect with our Heavenly Father to release our thanksgiving and praise to Him that was not within the thinking realm. I am not talking about something mysterious as we have been led to believe our imagination is, but it is real even though it can not be accessed by the five physical senses. By using our imagination, we can bridge the gap between what is seen with what is unseen. In doing so we can enter into the spiritual realm with a more meaningful worship.

Here again, we must practice restraint with our imagination. King Solomon states in Proverbs 6:18 about one of the seven things the Lord hates- "a heart that devises wicked imagination." And in 2 Corinthians 10:5 KJV: it says, "Casting down imaginations, and every high thing that exalteth itself against the knowledge of God, and bringing into captivity every thought to the obedience of Christ." Our imagination must be kept pure!

What is a wicked imagination? We can allow our minds to wander into an area of wickedness by our emotions when we feel we are being ignored, misunderstood, angered, hurt, or slighted. We may secretly hope others will fail, or start planning ways of getting even or destroying the individual. These things can become rooted in the heart and grow into all sorts of evilness. In Mark 7:20-23: Jesus says, "What comes out of a man is what makes him 'unclean.' For from within, out of men's hearts, come evil thoughts, sexual immorality, theft, murder, adultery, greed, malice, deceit, lewdness, envy, slander, arrogance, and folly. All these evils come from inside and make man unclean." These imaginative thoughts must be cast down. Forgiveness is a tool we can choose to root out evil imaginations from our hearts. Again, think about what you are thinking, and why you are thinking that!

Many marriages would still be intact if the imaginations of one or both partners had cast down the imagination of what it would be like to be with someone else. Pornographers would not have a market to make millions and a platform to destroy relationships by distorting reality. The mind uses the pornographic images to create sexually stimulating scenes, a compulsion to repeat the scene with more graphic details, and thus creates a strong addiction to the pornography. If continued, this compulsive desire may demand to be acted out physically on an innocent victim. Stop before a crime is committed! Seek God's forgiveness, repent, and be accountable to a trusted person! Respect for the created female or male will serve to tame this seemingly harmless desire.

The same is true with movies and other media outlets that play on people's imagination to do evil or to distort reality. It all starts with imagination then thinking on that image and later acting out what has been imagined. Be aware of fantasies portrayed in the media which feed our desires and attitudes for having an unrealistic world where the syndrome, "and they lived happily ever after," exists. Good and evil are in the power of the tongue, as well as the powerful images we develop in our minds. Again, we must choose to allow only Godly images of reality to remain in our minds.

This unrestrained imagination was grievous to our Lord. In Genesis 6:5&6 KJV: "And God saw that the wickedness of man was great in the earth, and that every imagination of thoughts of his heart was only evil continually. And it repented the Lord that he had made man on the earth, and it grieved him at his heart." How could the created grieve the Creator? Notice it was not just a few imaginations, but

every imagination of thoughts of his heart was **only** evil continually! And thus, the judgement of the flood was pronounced on the earth.

What if you are the object of someone else's imagination and he/she thinks you did or said something he/she only imagined! Evidence may help prove your innocence, but there is not always evidence to the contrary to what is imagined. What can you do? Make sure your intentions and behaviors are well understood. This requires clear communications and staying away from compromising situations. Abstain from all appearances of evil to protect yourself from being falsely accused. Be aware of others who may have an overactive, vain imagination, or are under the influence of mind altering drugs.

Input from the five senses, sight, smell, hearing, taste, and touch gives much real information to the brain for interpretation to help us maneuver in our environment, as well as releasing a plethora of emotions. We rely on these senses for safety, discernment, and protection while the emotional interpretation drives our feelings, responses, or reactions to others. We are social creatures seeking love, affection, and affirmation!

Failure to Thrive is a syndrome that occurs when an infant does not receive enough touch or social input from his/her mother or caretaker. The human touch, cuddling, hugs, and interaction with the child is a must for the infant to thrive. Also, the child's brain develops better with this loving interaction which causes the attachment hormone, oxytocin, to be released from the brain. Touch is important to each of us. Socializing with a handshake or an embracing hug conveys feelings of honor, love, concern, or empathy. During this time of "social distancing" is having detrimental effects on adults as well as children and teens! The profound impact may not be known for some time!

Our eye gate allows the brain to interpret what we see in the world. "Beauty is in the eye of the beholder" is a cliche well known to us, but it is the interpretation of that "beauty" that the brain makes that makes it beautiful (*Beauty is*). We cannot always shield ourselves from what we momentarily see, but gazing takes more time. King David probably would not have fallen into sin with

Bathsheba if he would have looked away, but he watched her bathing! (2 Samuel 11). Psalms 119:37 NLT: "Turn my eyes from worthless things, and give me life through your word." Is that why pornography and illicit sexual activity are so detrimental to our being, since the same additive neurotransmitters are released from the brain and make the behavior addicting?

The ear gate allows interpretation of sounds, voices, nature, or alarms. Music has a wonderful effect on the developing brain and the adult brain by producing feel good hormones. The psychological effects enhance learning, intelligence, concentration, and memory. Ever notice how easy it is to remember facts if set to music? Music therapy is used to repair the injured brain from accident, stroke, or aging. Slow tempo and low pitched music calm stressful emotions and irrational behaviors. A story told in I Samuel 16:14-23 tells of the tormented King Saul who would call David to play on his harp to calm his spirit. In verse 23-b: "Then relief would come to Saul; he would feel better, and the evil spirit would leave him." Over a dozen times we are told anyone with ears to hear should listen and understand what the Spirit has to say. 2 Timothy 4:3 NLT warns us: "For the time is coming when people will no longer listen to sound and wholesome teaching. They will follow their own desires and will look for teachers who will tell them whatever their itching ears want to hear." We must watch what we allow into our being through our ear gate. This is so important in our day!

The sense of taste and smell are somewhat related. The brain receives the chemical message of taste for interpretation from the front and back tongue, roof and sides of mouth: sweet, sour, salt, bitter, or savory. This message may be pleasurable or not, it may be for protection as sensing too hot or may alert us of danger as in poisonings or spoiled foods. Smell relays information to the brain sensed by preceptors in the nose and through the mouth. Different odors have a distinct meaning to each of us. We create a memory for taste and odors. Have you ever noticed that certain odors remind you of a person or place? Oh to be able to develop a taste for our Lord as David did! Psalms 34:8 NLT says: "Taste and see that the Lord is good. Oh the joys of those who take refuge in Him." And 119:103: "How sweet your words to my taste."

How delightful our senses make this life! What about that special touch, that first kiss, that favorite dessert, on and on I could go. But, we again must keep what God has made for our enjoyment by keeping God first, no idols, no illicit passions, no impurities, no substance abuse, or overindulgence. Here we get a chance to practice self control by stopping the brain from building powerful, addictive tastes and imaginations through our senses.

Our thinking may be influenced by others, our emotions or our experiences. Whether it be our parents, teachers, professors, spiritual leaders or coworkers, all tend to be an influence for good or bad. Included in this influence are media, movies, books, and more. Do we ever have our own thoughts? We so often think we originate the thought on our own. Be on guard! We have an enemy that may inject his influence into our minds for our destruction or for the destruction of others. Then the enemy convinces us that the thought was our own.

How then should we think? I think the only safe way is to become immersed in the Word of God and allow the Holy Spirit to police our minds. Often I need to talk to myself, telling myself what I am going to imagine or not going to imagine, think or not think. It is so easy to let other things influence our thinking.

How do we have the mind of Christ? Romans 12:2&3: "Do not conform any longer to the pattern of this world, but be transformed by the renewing of your mind. Then you will be able to test and approve what God's will is- his good, pleasing, and perfect will." By devouring God's word, we immerse into Christ, taking on His character, pushing out the world and living in truth, reacting in love, and with wisdom. This requires devoted time and energy to study and to expose our minds to meaningful and truthful facts of life. The choice is ours. Allowing just anything entrance into the mind is not wise. The Word of God is the guideline for knowledge and truth and the Word can be trusted. "And be constantly renewed in the spirit of your mind (having a fresh mental and spiritual attitude). And put on the new nature (the regenerate self) created in God's, (Godlike) in true righteousness and holiness." Ephesians 4:23&24. Amplified.

One of the saddest diagnoses I've had to deal with is suicide or attempted suicide. There are numerous reasons for wanting to end this precious life. The victims often see no other way out of their situation, mental illness may be the causative factor, or they may be acting on an impulse. The clinically depressed or those in physical agony may render them incompetent to make rational decisions. Drugs, legal and illegal, and alcohol may also be the culprit and cloud one's rational thinking.

Suicide has risen for the past 20 years, the highest rate is in the 45-54 age groups and in the elderly (*Transforming the Treatment*). During the COVID-19 pandemic, Centers for Disease Control report 25.5 % of 18-24 age group seriously considered suicide in the month of May, 2020 (*Covid- 19*). Teens and young people have not had enough experiences to completely develop their frontal lobe of the brain which allows them to relate cause and effects of behaviors and the resultant consequences. Thus, they react, instead of thinking of the outcomes of their behaviors which results in the frequency of deaths from suicide. In any event, the suffering of the friends and family members is beyond comprehension. Much compassion needs to be extended to friends and to the family.

Years ago, I felt the need to have answers to suicide. I believe the Lord showed me something simple as He usually does. If we are a spirit, we have a soul and we live in a body - suicide is the termination of the body. It is my belief if the person has invited Jesus into his/her heart then commits suicide, his/her eternity with Jesus is assured. Jesus died for all our sins, past, present, and future. Let God be the judge.

There are many reasons one may commit suicide. We may feel that we would never commit suicide, but that may not be the case. The brain is subject to emotional and physical changes that affect his/her thinking which may make rational thinking momentary impossible. Hallucinations, delusions, and other disorders may be in control, not their rational thinking. And then there is our enemy, the devil, who likes to confuse, as well as, lie about the self-worth of distraught individuals.

Ms. Beaver was a middle aged, depressed patient who had tried to commit suicide numerous times before this admission. Her family was exhausted and perplexed with her behaviors. After developing a rapport with her, I asked her how she felt before the attempt and what was she thinking. "I don't remember thinking anything, a voice always tells me to do it."

I replied gently, "Do you know you do not have to obey every voice that comes into your head telling you to harm yourself?"

She looked at me shocked, "I don't have to obey the voice?"

"No," I replied, "Just tell the voice, 'I refuse to listen to you and I will not kill myself!'" She seemed relieved to know she could make that choice to refuse to listen to "the voice". I challenged her to repeat that statement every time the voice came to her.

I followed her progress for a while and she did not attempt suicide again. We must be aware, "The thief (Satan) comes only to steal and kill and destroy; I (Jesus) have come that they may have life, and have it to the full." John 10:10. Note, Satan comes to steal our peace, rational thinking, or sanity first, gaining entrance into our minds, then he brings death and destruction.

Changing a person's way of thinking is a mammoth task. Feelings of depression, hopelessness, and despair become all too familiar to him/her; change can be painful. Perhaps we should do as King David did. Speak to our soul, tell it what to think! Replace negative thoughts with at least three positive ones. Also, change what we are saying as "I am just depressed." "There is no hope because bad things will always happen to me." Speaking negative things gives our enemy the right to attack us. Remember, our enemy can not read our mind. We tell him everything he needs to know by the words of our mouth, attitudes, and our behaviors! Don't give up, keep trying, your breakthrough may be just around the corner.

Before we allow a mind-set of thoughts to take root, it would be wise to run the "thought" by the Spirit's approval. "We take captive every thought to make it obedient to Christ." 2nd Corinthians 10:5. It is amazing how many people do not think about what they are thinking! The first rule is to make sure the information is correct. Our society seems to be couched in lies, half-truths, rumors, and deceit. Another rule for thinking is a command: "Whatever is true, whatever is noble, whatever is right, whatever is pure, whatever is lovely, whatever is admirable...if anything is excellent or praiseworthy...**think** about such things." Philippians 4:8. Notice; we are told to "think" not to rely on our emotions. By allowing our spirits to be led by the Holy Spirit and to police our thought life, will save us from much depression, deception, and despair.

The Will

To me, the "free will" God gave man was risky. He knew man very well, but His love for man out weighed the risk. I suppose it is a little like our desire to have children. We knew they might disappoint us, but we loved them even before they were conceived and wanted them so desperately.

This "will" allows us to tenaciously stick by the decisions we have made. I have witnessed people who have incredible "intestinal fortitude" and can withstand unbelievable amounts of emotional, physical pain or distress and still remain positive. How do they do it? They have a remarkable will to survive and to thrive. They are determined to press ahead in the face of adversity without any fear.

There is something that happens in us when we state, "I will." Our will is a part of our decision making ability apart from any emotional input. When we use our will to make a decision, it may seem sterile, cold, and devoid of any emotions. In a courtroom, "I will" is stated to declare our intentions to follow a declaration. This is the "I will" our Creator was searching for in His risky endeavor to find a people who would freely love and serve Him.

Our will may be in submission to another's will. God gave us a free will; care should be taken to be protective of this gift. Others may try to dictate their will or desires upon us. Often it is to our destruction. Mind altering substances or even powerful influencers have destroyed many lives when a person submits his/her will to them. Toxic relationships develop as we abandon our own will to another person's will. This frequently happens in dependent - codependent relationships. Again, I cannot stress how vitality important it is to have the Holy Spirit's direction in making decisions and in living our lives.

On the night of His betrayal, Jesus gave us a perfect example of submission in this prayer: "Father, if you are willing, please take away this cup of suffering from me. But I want your will, not mine." Luke 21:22. He so trusted His Heavenly Father, He was willing to endure beatings, the cross, and the shame. Since God cannot look upon sin, He knew God would have to turn His face away from Him for the first time as the sin of the world was laid upon Him. Ultimately, Jesus knew He could submit His will to the Heavenly Father because He had total trust in Him.

Another statement of Jesus's promise in John 6:37 NLT: "However, those the Father has given me will come to me, and I will never reject them." And later on Jesus was comforting His disciples in 13:1: "When everything is ready, I will come and get you, so that you will always be with me where I am." Now that is a promise on which we can depend! It is God's will that none should be lost; all that is needed is for mankind to submit his will to the Father's will.

We have already read how Miss Kitty used her will to prolong her life in order to see her grandson and to later decide it was time to die. I believe we have more responsibility and control of our life than I previously thought.

Yes, God is sovereign, but He has given the keys to the kingdom to us as believers. Matthew 16:19 NLT: "And I will give you the key to the Kingdom of Heaven, whatever you forbid on earth will be forbidden in heaven, and whatever you permit on earth will be permitted in heaven." WOW, when we realize that; it changes everything! How else could free will operate unless we were allowed to use our free will to speak to a situation for a change?

So many times Jesus admonished us to just speak to our problems, consistently, and firmly to see a change. Earlier in an airplane incident, I was begging God to help and nothing was changing. Things changed when I asked Jesus how to pray and He told me! Jesus wants us to ask Him! Jesus spoke to the fig tree and it dried up and again He said we could, "say to the mountain to throw yourself into the sea and it will be done." Matthew 21-22. In John 14:14 NLT: "Yes, ask me anything in my name and I will do it." We are not told to beg God, but to ask in faith then speak over a situation in the name of Jesus!

When it is necessary for us to ask others for forgiveness for our offense, do so, no strings attached, no excuses, no blame! This offense may not have been mostly our fault, but it is a feeling unlike no other to still ask for forgiveness. "I am sorry, I was wrong, please forgive me." "What can I do to make it right?" These are great scripts to remember!

The *will* is paramount when making forgiveness possible to those that have offended us. "But I do not feel like forgiving them." "They have not asked for my forgiveness". "Look what they did to me!" Those are some of the arguments for not forgiving. You decided to forgive! The offender may never ask you to forgive him/her. Exercise your will! You declare forgiveness for him/her anyway, verbally if necessary and pray for them, asking God to bless him/her! Praying for your offender is a sure way of changing your attitude towards him/her. This may take a while to work through but it is worth it. The feelings will come later. I promise!

Often we refuse to forgive thinking it will absolve their offense against us. Not so, forgiveness allows us to be free from the offender and the offense! Forgiveness given to others will prevent negative emotions like bitterness, anger, revenge, and resentment from taking root in our heart. These toxic emotions may contribute to physical conditions such as high blood pressure, stroke, immunodeficiency, headache, and changes in the body's chemistry. Some of the mental and social effects include depression, anxiety, shame, self-loathing, regret, and relationship failures. All this can be prevented if we exercise our will to love, determine in our hearts to forgive, and decide to practice self-control where our emotions are concerned.

Our will is necessary when we attempt to practice self-control. Self-control is an act we do on purpose out of our determination to change our attitudes or behaviors. If we do not manage our emotions, emotions will manage us. Self-control involves the whole being, spirit, soul, and body with the will leading the way in decision making. It takes listening to your spirit for knowledge and wisdom, to make intelligent and compassionate decisions of the soul, and a healthy body will naturally follow. The Creator gave us a will to steer our decisions so that we can live our lives in a healthy, balanced, and peaceful manner.

When the *will* is used for evil, others suffer. Hitler is a good example of too much unrestrained power allowing pride, arrogance and deceit to control him. In his quest to make the master race, he hijacked the will of others, causing them to commit all kinds of atrocities. I am sure he felt he was in control of his own destiny and he was for a while. In the end, history reveals him to be quite different than what he thought himself to be. His self-deception, wrong thinking, combined with his will to make his country a pure race resulted in much destruction. "Pride goes before destruction, a haughty spirit before a fall." Proverbs 16:18.

Amazing, is it not? The power he had over others to do his will. It has been known, he was into the occult. The desire for power over others is so compelling in some individuals. Satan is always looking for an entrance to set up a stronghold, usually through pride. It is wise to take inventory of individuals in our lives that may be trying to influence or control us for their own cause. Knowing God's word and having the Holy Spirit's guidance within us may protect us from getting trapped in this type of delusion.

Is it possible to change someone else's will? If we force our will onto him/her, that would be controlling them. This plot is used by many in the cults, political movements, and unfortunately by overzealous Christian parents in dealing with their rebellious young people. We can not change his/her will, but God can! When we operate in God's Spirit, we do not use the same methods as the world uses. We may ask our Lord to have the individual's will to line up with what God's will is for that person. What are the weapons that are available to us when Satan has established such a stronghold in their life?

Love and prayer! First, make sure you are not operating in a prideful or selfish attitude. Go to God first for wisdom; ask Him for ways of showing love. Declare the ungodly plans or evil influences to fail in their life; pray for loving Christians to minister to them; and pray for what to say or not to say to them. Pray their eyes will be opened to God's truth! Pray they will develop a disdain for the way they are going. Prayer is tough love! The closer we are to someone; the harder it is for us to be an effective witness to them using words. In 2 Corinthians 10:3-5 we are told: "For though we live in the world, we do not wage war as the world does. The weapons we fight with are not like the weapons of the world. On the contrary, they have divine power to demolish strongholds. We demolish arguments and every pretension that sets itself up against the knowledge of God, and we take captive every thought to make it obedient to Christ." This takes time, dedication, energy, and love.

The world's response may be, "He/she made their bed, let him/her lie in it"; or "It was his/her decision." That may be true, but love is not willing to accept the world's ways. God's love is so high and wide, it is far above anything the world comprehends. To operate in God's love, we must know the Father God intimately, be willing to crucify our flesh, and crush our own pride. In other words, we must be willing to pour ourselves out for someone else. Suppose that someone still does not change after a long, long time? Stand, and having done all to stand, stand! This is a test of endurance for those who will intercede for others in prayer.

The mother, Mrs. Fox, for years prayed for her son to receive Jesus Christ as his Lord and Savior. She was faithful to pray even though it looked as if it would never happen and it did not happen in her lifetime. But God is faithful when prayers are spoken! It took a drastic event like cardiac arrest, death, and going to hell to get his attention. The first time I witnessed the way of salvation to him, he had allowed a long-time stronghold of sin to develop in his heart which was preventing him from being responsive to God's loving call. All the while, Jesus took care of the stronghold rather easily. All he had to do was ask and to submit his will to Jesus! God can take what seems so pleasurable, shine the light of truth on it, and it loses its pull and intrigue on us. Keep praying no matter what the situation looks like. What if Mrs. Fox had given up and said he was hopeless or he had gone too far. I believe Satan would have won!

Make God's will your will. This will make for a stress free life filled with joy, peace, and love as we are content to trust our Heavenly Father. You will face difficulties, disappointments, and discouragement in life, but realizing the Father's direction and unfailing love will see us through to a victory. Know God's will as revealed in the Bible, choose to follow His will, and when you miss the mark, be quick to repent, admit error, and reestablish your relationship with the Father.

The Emotions

Emotions are made up of our feelings either high, low, or serene. What would we do without them? Emotions are given to help us maneuver through this life, to bring happiness when we feel things are good, or to allow an outlet when we feel things are not so good. Again our feelings are controlled by whatever we think is going on around us at any specific time. When we are up; we are up; when we are down; we are down! When we are serene, we are peaceful, tranquil, and untroubled. Tranquility is boring to our youth because they have not yet acquired enough experiences for reflections. To the older generation, peace, tranquility, as well as time to reflect are all welcome.

Communication is the key to good emotional health. Too often we let our feelings depend on what we think others may have said or implied. Clear, precise communication skills are needed to understand what is being stated without the emotional slant. Often we may misinterpret what is said or implied by what we think it is, based on our past experiences. It may be our parents or our caretaker's voice we hear instead of what is actually being said. Practicing reflective communication helps both the speaker and the listener. To be a good communicator requires listening attentively, not thinking pridefully about "one upping" the speaker, which usually results in an interruption of the speaker. When threatened, "What am I going to say in defense of myself," blocks our ability to hear. Effective listening skills are more than just being quiet; it is active listening!

Did you know that tears are medicinal? Tears contain a certain "feel good" agent in them. Is that why we feel better after a good cry (Pullman, *Three Types*)? We better not rely on crying too often or we will deplete our tear reserve and weary those around us who have listening ears! Are you thinking about someone who turns to tears to get attention or sympathy? It is fun to watch children do this, but as adults it is not amusing. I call this crying, tearless crying. Real tears, coming from a heart in the agony of brokenness do have medicinal value. Our Creator thought of our emotional pain and planned a way for comfort!

Emotions were never given to be the plumb line for making the many decisions that come our way in this life. Our perception of what others think of us elicit a plethora of emotions which may or may not be true. Positive, realistic, encouraging reinforcement of one's ability is a must for our healthy emotional development. How we feel about ourselves influences our attitudes and decision making abilities. Often goals are reached because we feel they are attainable; conversely, goals are not reached because we feel they are not attainable. Our success in life will be stymied by incorrect perception of who we are, either inflated, prideful or inadequate and demoralized.

Jealousy and envy flourish with feelings of inferiority and inadequacy. To be envious is to believe you have not received what you thought you deserved, wanted, or that you were not treated fairly. Jealousy is to feel someone else is trying to take what is yours or to steal another's affection from you. Both of these emotions are toxic and when coupled with uncontrolled anger are the making for a disastrous situation. If left unchecked, these toxic emotions will cause repressed anger to result in paranoia, resentment, hatred of others, or even murder. Being thankful and having a heart of gratitude for what you do have is a perfect solution to envy and jealousy. Realizing the responsibility that possessions carry should lessen envy. Jealousy and over possessiveness in a relationship will certainly destroy it!

Guilt over wrongdoings may weigh us down and inadvertently cause repetitive greater wrongdoings. If not dealt with in a timely manner, guilt leads to shame. Own up to the behavior! Do not blame others or make excuses. The English poet and essayist, Alexander Pope said, "To err is human; to forgive, divine (Pope, *To err*)." Ask God for forgiveness, accept His forgiveness, repent, and ask others who were offended to forgive you. False guilt results when another person projects his/her guilt upon you. This results in much pain and confusion, but God can bring clarity and healing just for the asking. Again, guard your heart from false guilt.

Shame causes such a painful feeling of distress and humiliation. Someone, usually an authoritative figure, says something or does something to destroy our opinion of ourselves. The caustic, hurtful words of a parent or caregiver leave the child helpless to interpret his/her world. The rational thinking in the brain's frontal lobe has not fully developed which leaves the child to react emotionally. This powerful negative emotional reaction may last throughout adulthood.

An example of this is childhood sexual abuse which steals the innocence of the child. This sinful act carries a heavy price tag of guilt and shame. The perpetrator will not pay the price of guilt, so it falls on the innocent child to pay in the form of "false" guilt. Then the child may carry this false guilt all of his/her lifetime. The journey to wholeness for those who are victims of childhood sexual abuse begins when he/she realizes the power of God to heal their brokenness. Recognize it was the enemy who stole his/her innocence and give the false guilt to Jesus. The journey continues by permitting God's unconditional love to change the way he/her perceives himself/herself and cleanses his/her emotions of negative thoughts. Forgiveness is a powerful healing tool! Freedom can be attained by making a decision to forgive the perpetrator and leaning on God for strength to do so. Feelings of forgiveness will happen later.

That is why God gave us reasoning and thinking ability. By listening to others talk, you can tell if they are led by thinking or by simply their emotions. In discussions they will say "I think thus and so;" however, if emotions are leading, they will say, "I feel like it is thus and so." A serene approach to decision making incorporates both facets by thinking it through and then permitting an emotional response to make it more palpable!

What happens when we just react emotionally? The way we let ourselves feel releases neurotransmitters/hormones (stress hormone) in response to a fact or perceived fact. Example, a big black bear that crosses the path ahead sends messages of danger to the brain. It's now fight or flight time. The sympathetic nervous system releases numerous neurotransmitters/hormones to cause the body to be on high alert for survival. Some of the physical responses of the body include: the bronchi in the lungs dilate to allow more air in, muscles call up stored glucose for energy consumption, heart rate speeds up, pupils dilate for added light and the blood pressure elevates in an attempt to provide the necessary energy for fight or flight. These hormones make us "feel afraid" but fight or flight may be the wrong choice.

While in the Alaskan wilderness, we met a native who told me about a confrontation he had with a grizzly bear when he was doing a documentary on wildlife. He was alone on his assignment and carrying his camera gear. Suddenly, an upright grizzly bear appeared on his path! All the feelings of flight appeared also! He knew he was a dead man. A grizzly can run half of a football field in three seconds or about forty miles per hour. He was well aware of this so he stood still, refusing to panic by calming his emotions. He decided to start snapping pictures of the bear so his family would know what happened to him if the camera was ever found.

As the bear approached, he looked curiously at the camera, grabbed it from his hands and ran off into the thicket. I guess the grizzly was camera shy! What happened to the camera? He was certainly not going to search for it! If he allowed himself to panic and run, he would be a dead man. Bears do love chasing their main entrées.

We met a young lady in the Grand Teton National Park who told this story of her confrontation with a black bear. She knew running was not an option although all her senses told her to take flight. So she fell to the ground as if she were dead. The bear sniffed, walked around her curiously, then grabbed her straw hat and ran off with it. She had scars of the claw marks on her scalp to prove it!

She thought that act would work as black bears like their prey not only dead but on the aged side also. She planned to escape as soon as he left. It worked for her but it is not recommended by the experts for survival. Standing still, waving arms to make yourself appear larger, making noise while facing the bear without direct eye contact is recommended as a survival skill (Bortschiller, *Staying Safe)*. I think she actually fainted, so would I!

Likewise a perceived danger can cause the same kind of reaction within the body as real danger. Worrying about things that may or may not happen is to feed fear into the situation giving it the power over you. Jesus again had much to say about worrying in Matthew 6:25-34: "(You) take no thought about what you should eat or drink." Break that habit of saying, "I am worried about this or that happening." The physical body doesn't know the difference in real and perceived danger unless we consciously tell it. Constant worrying causes a cascade of stress hormones to be released and sustained. Chronic worrying is a bad habit and can be broken by replacing it by thinking good positive thoughts.

As it has been said, it takes at least 21 days to create a habit and at least 21 days to break a habit. However, a thought of "worry" must be replaced with a positive thought and verbalized for this to be accomplished.

Words replace thoughts. So much of what we worry about never materializes, anyway. This chronic tension throughout the body, causes much damage to the vascular system and vital organs, not to mention premature aging.

Similar reaction occurs during anger. Our blood pressure goes up, heart races, muscles are empowered by glucose conversion, the lungs' passageways dilate and our defense mechanism is now on high alert. Note, I did not say our brain was thinking clearly; it is simply in a reactionary mode. Regrettably, that's why we say things in haste. Again, our bodies cannot tolerate this sustained state for long, something has to give. If allowed to persist, the individual alienates friends, family, and cannot form lasting relationships. Some may enjoy this "high" and blame others for making them angry. However, no one can make us angry; we choose to be angry ourselves! It is a choice. "A quick-tempered man does foolish things, and a crafty man is hated." Proverbs 14:17.

Apostle Paul addresses this in his letter to the Ephesians 4:26-27: "In your anger do not sin. Do not let the sun go down while you are still angry, and do not give the devil a foothold."

Notice he did not say to not get angry, but do not hold on to anger. If the devil's foothold is enough to make you sin, how does he do it? By having access into your life he can deceive you. Get rid of thoughts like: "Who do they think they are?" or "It was not my fault, Look what they did to me." or "Just wait, I will get even with them." Controlling anger is the mark of a mature man or woman. Our society seems to be steeped in uncontrollable anger. Crime rates bear this out as statistics show.

How do we control our anger; it just feels so good to just let it fly! First of all, stop saying, "When I get mad, I just let it fly," or "I just can't help myself." Sure, we all feel like that! Stop wearing anger as a badge of honor. You are only deceiving yourself if you do. The sympathetic nervous system gives us an addictive rush when we are angry but to be truly successful in life, we must learn how to practice restraint. Consider this, one minute of anger weakens the immune system for 4-5 hours, while one minute of laughter boosts the immune system up to 24 hours! Learn to laugh! Laughter is the best medicine after all.

Prolonged chronic stress causes the adrenal glands to excrete cortisol, the main stress hormone. This hormone has receptor sites throughout the body and affects most of its systems. Cortisol prolongs the fight and flight state leading to heart disease, insulin resistance, carbohydrate craving, depression, brain shrinkage, suppressed immunology, and cognitive difficulties.

We are equipped with another system to counteract the sympathetic system (fight or flight). That is the parasympathetic system (rest or digest). Keeping things in balance is the key to a balanced life. This must be the peace and tranquillity input.

The tenth cranial nerve, or the vagus, is the longest, wandering cranial nerve within the body. It provides communication between the core part of the body and the brain. Some refer to it as being responsible for the "gut level feeling" we may experience. Feeling satisfied after eating, enjoying favorite foods and someone's company are some of them. The vagus nerve calms the body and emotions (rest or digest).

The vagus nerve can be activated by doing controlled, restrained, slow deep breathing to calm the physical body, the emotions, and allow the mind to process more clearly when in distress. Remembering to do this is my problem! After doing deep breathing exercises, pray a short prayer, "Help me, Jesus" or "I trust you Jesus!" It is also beneficial to ask the Lord what He wants to show you about the incident. It is amazing what can be learned, problems solved, or understood by just asking. "Everyone should be quick to listen, slow to speak, and slow to become angry." James 1:19.

This technique is also helpful in calming oneself before and during public speaking. Fear and anxiety during public speaking can be paralyzing emotions which can cause a brain freeze, sweaty palms and racing heart. After practicing this relaxing technique over time public speaking may become easier.

Breathing techniques will help temporarily but deeper emotions must be dealt with to erase the feelings such as inferiority or inadequacy. Stop comparing yourself to others and realize you are created uniquely in the image of a God, and receive God's unconditional love in your heart. We must strive to be alert to the signs and symptoms of these negative emotions just as we would be alert to a devastating disease. Avoid dwelling on negative, toxic emotions and attitudes, such as greed, bitterness, hatred, self pity, hurt, or loneliness. Tear down these strongholds by meditating on Scriptures, seek forgiveness and forgive others, develop a concern and love for others, and claim God's promises to help control negative emotions. Recognize and deal these negative emotions early before these strongholds develop. Be ready to love!

We have already discussed one of the four Greek terms for love, *agape*. This is the God kind of love which is given to us at the time our spirits are born again by God. *Agape* love enhances love when it is applied in concert with these three other types of love. Of course the secular world can "love," but there is a deeper, more sincere, and more enjoyable facet of the pure unconditional love available to us through God.

Philia is the love between friends which is based on affection and it can be a strong, compelling love (Lewis, *Four Greek*). Jesus demonstrated this love at the gravesite of Lazarus when He saw the sorrow of Mary and Martha. "Jesus wept." John 11:35. Empathy for others can only be expressed when we lay aside our selfishness, self-seeking attitudes, and then we can truly love. John 15:13 explains: "Greater love has no one than this, that he lay down his life for his friends." This is the ultimate in pure love. It has no fear of what others say, think, or feel or what it will cost us. It is unlike the narcissistic, egotistical love of oneself that serves itself for what it can get out of others. The way we love, showing it by caring for our friends, defines who we are. The more we practice walking in love, the more we are able to love and love flows freely from us.

Storge is the special bond between brothers, sisters, mother, father and grandparents. Brothers and sisters in the Lord are often included in this type of love (Lewis *Four Greek*). The Apostle Paul often refers to this type of love in his writings as he makes reference to them as brothers and sisters in the Lord. This is so true. With God as our Father, we truly are brothers and sisters! It is all in the family! Another reason for this strong bond may be physiological. The neurotransmitter oxytocin is released from the brain during pregnancy, birth, and during nursing that causes the infant and mother to bond. We see this in nature. Have you ever tried to separate a calf, kittens, or puppies from their mothers? The mother hippo risks her own life and hides her male baby hippo from the father who might kill it! God provided this attachment syndrome to protect the young and to protect the bonds of marriage.

Eros refers to romantic love or sexual attraction (Lewis, *Four Greek*). In our Western culture, we often "fall in love" magically with some eternal soulmate. Again all kinds of hormones come in to play when physical attraction occurs. The feeling of "being in love" is so exhilarating, mind blowing, and passionate that all caution may be thrown to the wind. This feeling is a result of the release of serotonin, (mood elevator) vasopressin and oxytocin, (attachment developer) dopamine and norepinephrine (reward, fulfillment, and happiness). Those who fall in love in a moment of passion, often fall out of love just as readily when those hormones subside. Unfortunately, this is the love that most of our society thinks is real! When the appeal and excitement of the relationship wanes, broken commitments, broken hearts, broken dreams, and broken lives occur. No reasoning or thinking is involved, just reactions to the chemicals that are excreted. Emotions are given for our enjoyment, not given to us as a foundation for making lasting relationships.

The neurotransmitter, oxytocin, is released automatically by the brain during intimacy of a man and a woman. This is part of God's plan to make the two become one! All sexual relationships create some kind of a bond, but the bond becomes weaker and weaker as it moves between multiple partners. Only God's forgiveness can break the bonds of memory and restore health to our brain and emotions when multiple partners have been involved. So ask Jesus for forgiveness, repent, and receive His wonderful forgiveness.

Remember, our systems cannot sustain high passions for a long time. Lasting love must be built on something more substantial to endure the hardships of marriage. That foundation is found in 2 Corinthians 6:14: "Do not be yoked together with unbelievers. For what do righteousness and wickedness have in common? Or what fellowship can light have with darkness?" Our Father is waiting to have input so the marriage and children may have harmonious, healthy homes. Commitment to another takes an act of the mind and will. A decision must be made to cherish, love, be patient, kind, generous, be able to forgive and to humbly say, "I am so sorry." This decision also involves a determination to stick it out when things are tough. Make the decision first, make allowance for each other, nourish the marriage, and crucify selfishness. With God leading, this is where real love grows and flourishes.

Our concept of marriage is failing currently! The divorce rate is disappointingly high and even more couples are living together without the bonds of marriage. Some divorced individuals have admitted to me they regretted their divorce. You know the "20/80" rule sometimes applies here. The new attraction has 20% more of the excitement and appeal that the old partner did not have; but sometime after the divorce, it is discovered the new partner lacks 80% of the qualities of the discarded partner

(*Habit Formation*) This is something one should consider, if entertaining plans for divorce. For these reasons, marriage should be treated with honor, respect, and as a serious commitment before the Lord. Before marriage, couples should discuss and then settle questions such as how to manage money, debt, household tasks, extended family, and their desire for children and how many. We prepare ourselves for all other contractual agreements, why not for the all-important marriage contract? The most important question for the Christian is, what is his/her partner's relationship with the Lord?

Keep your marriage vibrant! Love your mate unselfishly! All Satan needs is a slight flirtation from a third party to sow a seed of discontent. Be aware of this temptation! It is easier to stop at this point than it will be later when the momentary passion hijacks your marriage. Is it the excitement of the "forbidden activity" that is fueling your boring life? If so, work at making your own life and marriage exciting, adventurous, and fun once again. God sets boundaries in marriage to protect you and your mate. Allow Jesus to take control of your emotions, fill any voids, and place Him at the center of your marriage. Do not expect your mate to fulfill the needs that only the Lord can do.

Another trap that destroys a marriage occurs when one partner worships the other. The one being worshiped will soon despise the one doing the worshipping. The worshiper becomes eaten up with jealousy and bitterness leading to more possessiveness. Physical abuse and emotional abuse may occur. God knew we would become like what we worship! Humans are not capable of being worshipped for any length of time! The worshipper will be detested by the one being worshipped! Insanity develops with human worship. Hitler, Stalin, and some movie and rock stars are examples. God only deserves our worship!

Years ago, I had more answers for troubled marriages than I do now! By the time a couple shows up for counseling, one or both may have made up their minds to dissolve the marriage. Infidelity can be overcome with the help of prayer, counseling, time, patience, and much work from both parties. Trust is difficult to build back once it is broken. Accountability is a must! By seeking God with a passion, extending forgiveness to each other, and the determination to keep the marriage intact pays off with great dividends, especially if children are involved. Other grounds for a divorce is when domestic violence, or other criminal involvement is a factor. Escape! For those trapped in that relationship, it is not a marriage at all. Seek help for yourself and your children.

Once a young lady from an Eastern culture was asked how she could so easily submit to an arranged marriage. "How could I not? I know I am not old enough nor wise enough to make such an important decision so I must trust my parents." It might be wise for our culture to incorporate some parental advice or some trusted, wise counsel on this matter. Do we pride ourselves on independence a bit too much? Again, our Heavenly Father wants to be asked for His wisdom in choosing a mate!

Our society seems to allow emotions to rule their world. They want what they want when they want it, no waiting, no evaluation of facts, and little consideration of others! The consequences of their behavior has been justified or excused. The truth is lost in the sway of an emotional tide that is mostly devoid of facts. They thrive on their feelings instead of thinking on the truth.

Musical lyrics, poetry, literature, movies and theater thrive on finding erotic love or the drama associated with the lack of love. Our society is bombarded with emotional advertising to satisfy "my needs" to be, to have, to want more. Guard against self-centeredness. We all need love and acceptance. Permit the Lord to supply *agape* love and share it with others.

The Body

The most tangible part of our being is the body. It was formed from dust and will return to dust someday. If treated properly, it should last many, many years. The body's ability to take abuse from its owner is phenomenal! Lifespans throughout the centuries vary in length of time. Methuselah lived 969 years before the flood. Then Lord said, "My Spirit will not contend with man forever, for he is mortal, his days will be a hundred twenty years," Genesis 6:3. Could it be mankind's lifespan shortened due to the changes in the atmosphere after the flood? As the waters regressed, more ultraviolet rays from the sun permeated the earth. We know radiation speeds up the aging process. From 120 years, life expectancy fell as low as

30-40 years in the seventeen and eighteen centuries and slowly rose to today's highs of almost 78 years due to advances in modern medicine. I believe our Heavenly Father intervened and revealed to us medical knowledge so we could live long enough to rear the next generation and teach them the ways of God. That has always been the cry of God's heart! "So teach us to number our days, that we may apply our hearts unto wisdom." Psalms 90:12. KJV.

In infancy, our body was our world. It is amusing to watch an infant discover his/her hands. We really do not know much about the infant's ability to process his new world except when he is hungry, hurting, startled, cold, alone, or maybe in need of a diaper change. Then his body dictates attention. Later, he/she begins to interact with his/her environment with much anticipated smiles, coos, and giggles. A baby's limited social skills are rather instant, demanding, and totally self-serving. As he/she grows, the "give to me" phase adds a "do you see me" phase as the infant searches for his/her own identity and significance and later "may I help you" in adulthood. Crying and laughter are first responses to unpleasant or pleasant stimuli. We are told, Children laugh 300 times a day, adults 15-17 times per day (*Does a Laugh*). We adults should laugh more!

Laughter is a gift from our loving, thoughtful Heavenly Father. God knew this life on earth could be taxing, frustrating, and full of pain and hurt! He built into our physical bodies a pressure release valve to take care of those daily issues. Some cultures laugh more freely than ours. Why? It certainly is not because they have more conveniences than we have. In the African Bush, there is no electricity for heat, cooling, lighting, radios, TV, clocks, and forget charging your iPhone or iPad. There are no roads, just paths through the bush, no need for highways because they have no automobiles. Oh how they could laugh! I remember thinking how much they giggled and laughed as children do. They could see humor in almost everything. Perhaps that is why they were so endearing to me. Laughter allows us to bond with others, to love, to care without verbal communication.

Benefits of laughter makes us feel better because it reduces stress hormones, boosts the immune system by increasing infection fighting antibodies and thus increases resistance to disease. Another notable benefit is the release of endorphins from the brain which promotes a natural feeling of well-being and a temporary pain relief. The benefits of a good belly laugh lasts up to 45 minutes or longer and it can be contagious to those around us (Miller, *The Effects*). In addition to bringing people together, humorous statements have been known to even defuse conflicts.

Apparently, the body does not know the difference between spontaneous laughter and contrived laughter. That is to our advantage if we are needing a boost in our demeanor by spontaneous laughter. Laugh for no reason! Laughter is the body's physical response to a joyful, happy heart. Proverbs 17:22 Amp. says it best: "A happy heart is good medicine and a cheerful mind works healing, but a broken spirit dries up the bones." Bones are necessary to support our bodies and allow for our movement. Bones also manufacture the life giving blood cells within their marrow to promote a healthy body.

Smiling has some of the same effects on our well-being. A smile certainly can be contagious and is a way of showing friendliness. It is free, makes us feel better, and does not cause frown lines! Learning to smile first thing in the morning sets the mood for a good day. Make it a good habit to smile before getting out of bed, especially if awakening from a nightmare! A smile or chuckle to yourself can do wonders for a grumpy early morning attitude. Our Lord enjoys smiles and laughter. He designed us to laugh!

When we intentionally look upwards, it releases some feel good neurotransmitters from the brain. How interesting, our Heavenly Father knew that all along. That must be why the position of the head relays to others a body language without words. When we note the head is downcast, we think a person must be sad or even depressed. Now, a little common sense is required here. The person might be just looking where he/she is walking!

While being chased by his son Absalom, David declares in his prayer, "But you, O Lord, are a shield around me; you are my glory, the one who holds my head high." Psalms 3:3. David was reminding himself who his Lord is and I have to remind myself of that fact regularly to maintain my sanity and to keep my perspective on life. David knew God! David also knew that life gets in the way of our faith, making it weaker instead of stronger, unless we keep our focus on our Lord. By declaring to himself how the Lord provides, how He is glorious, and the lifter of his head. David encouraged himself.

Body language does tell us a lot about another's feelings or thinking. This is a skill that is developed over time, but caution is advised as it may, or may not be correctly interpreted. Some people are intuitively more developed in this area than others. We all know what a child's pouting sign means, but pouting does not look good on an adult! Some people think a pouting child is cute. My parents did not; they invited me to change that attitude or else. I knew what that meant! Pouting is a means of manipulating the parents to get what the child wants. On an adult, it is disguised more cleverly as a stern look, raised eyebrows, and by a swift turning away from the individual, then the silent treatment begins. Trying to control others in this manner shows immaturity of the individual and damages the relationship. "I want what I want and if I do not get it, you will pay!" Why not talk it out instead of wasting time pouting? Selfishness has to be denied if the relationship is to flourish.

Being aware of your own body language is helpful in business and interpersonal relationships. Years ago, I taught a class on this subject. It becomes necessary when dealing with hostile, angry, and afraid individuals to de-escalate a situation. People generally just want to be heard. When they feel threatened or feel you are incapable of handling a situation, their fears and hostility escalate. More than likely, they will misinterpret what is being said or done. Being able to control your emotions helps others to control their emotions; likewise, our out of control emotions escalate the negative emotions in others. "Like a city whose walls are broken down is a man who lacks self-control." Proverbs 25:28.

Nothing seems to be working, their anger is increasing, what do I do? Telling them to calm down is not the answer! Take a stance at a safe distance, allowing for space to take an extra step. Slightly leaning in towards the person shows your willingness to hear them. Use controlled breathing to calm yourself and pause briefly without an outward show of emotion. It may be necessary to repeat or rephrase what the hostile person has said to help you and the hostile person to understand the problem. Open hands convey openness, sincerity, and willingness or desire to help. (Note: This behavior started in the ancient days to show that no armor was hidden in the hands. Amusing, how these body languages are grounded in tangible truths). Also, a pleasant attitude with a slight tilting of the head shows interest and concern. Making statements like "How can I help?" or "Help me to understand what happened."

No making excuses, no tapping of fingers, shrugging shoulders, eye rolling or arms crossed over chest as that will convey defensiveness, impatience, rejection, or a disingenuous attitude. By lowering your voice if shouting is present and using pauses, may work wonders. Eye contact in our culture means honesty and politeness. However, in some Eastern cultures, they may see eye contact as aggressiveness or disdainfulness. Care should be taken in the interpretation of body language as it may have different meanings than what is assumed. However, body language can speak so loudly that it eschews what is being said.

Some years ago, we were touring in Lucerne, Switzerland with friends and we had crossed the wooden pedestrian Chapel Bridge to see the Lion Monument which commemorates the Swiss Guards who were massacred in the French Revolution. One of the travelers was sick that day and stayed behind in the hotel. I had gone back to the hotel to check on her and was returning via the bridge to the memorial in a downpour of rain. Since the bridge has a roof on it, I decided to bow down several times to get the rain out of the brim of my rain hat. To my astonishment, I was meeting a whole group of Japanese travelers, giggling and bowing repeatedly toward me in the traditional Japanese greeting. I just smiled at them as they stepped aside politely. I suppose they thought, "That is one friendly American!" When I was out of site, I started laughing to myself. Body language differs from culture to culture.

Another experience I had involved an incident that happened in the Philippines while on a church building mission. It was a hot, laborious endeavor high in the mountains. We had brought our own tank of water and plastic disposable cups. At the end of the day, I was gathering the trash at the site, crushing the cups, when I noticed a disapproving look on the face of a Filipino woman. I had seen that look before, when in a different culture, so I stopped what I was doing. After leaving the site, I watched them from a distance, I saw the ladies carefully stacking the uncrushed cups. They were taking our disposable cups to their homes to be used again. How embarrassing-my disposable American attitude was showing.

The body's amazing immune system causes inflammation in response to injury or infection in an attempt to heal itself. Our bodies do it automatically with increased blood flow and specialized white blood cells to the area which causes swelling, redness and pain. In response to infections, the immune system triggers a cascade of events of identifying the organism, to destroy it, and then building a system of recognition of the foreign invaders for future reference. However, problems occur when inflammation happens too rapidly or when it becomes chronic and the immune system attacks itself as the invader. This over activity is thought to be the cause of autoimmune diseases like lupus, scleroderma, multiple sclerosis, rheumatoid arthritis, thyroid disease, psoriasis, inflammatory bowel disease to name a few of the more than fifty autoimmune diseases. Chronic stress leads to changes in the cell's genes, bringing more inflammation. Some believe certain foods are responsible for inflammation while other foods are useful in calming the inflammation.

As I have stated, living under stress from negative emotions or disease takes a toll on our physical bodies. We are all aware of most of these physical conditions like heart disease, high blood pressure, headaches, tense muscles, insomnia, and digestive disorders. The immune system functions poorly under prolonged stress allowing frequent infections from pathogens or viruses to occur. Some stress is good as in small, incremental doses. How else would we be motivated to carry out the responsibilities of daily living? The culprit is when we remain in a stressful situation too long, either real or imagined, and become chronically stressed.

Not only does prolonged stress have a negative effect on the physical body, but it can result in mental and social disorders. Difficulty in thinking, agitated behaviors, inability to focus, poor judgment, worrying, anxiety, feelings of worthlessness and depression are just some of the symptoms. Any of these would definitely put a strain on relationships. Coping mechanisms between individuals vary greatly. Could that be because of learned behaviors or is it due to different physical abilities? I will let the psychology experts determine that.

The body is truly amazing! It has the natural ability to heal itself if we remove the causative factor in many cases. Also, some of the detrimental things we do to our bodies may be rectified by changes in the way we think and behave. A good example of this is the restoration of the body after cigarette smoking has stopped. The progress the body makes in its recovery in just 20 minutes to 20 years after smoking cessation is phenomenal *(WhyQuit)*. I have so much compassion and hope for those that are trying to quit smoking. I have seen the end damage of smoking and sadly the effects of secondhand smoke on the bodies of those that lived with the smoker.

Other addictions cause many detrimental effects on the body. Illegal drugs or some legal drugs for that matter and chronic alcohol abuse use causes profound changes in the brain and body. At first, changes in the brain include activation of the reward and pleasure systems within the brain, thus making the substance so appealing. Later, more of the substances are required to reach the same level of euphoria. Brain cells die and connections are damaged as the addiction progresses. Euphoria, now lost, but the need for excitement and calmness is intensified, but the damaged brain cannot deliver. The results are altered moods, slowed reflexes, loss of muscle tone, hormone imbalances, cloudy thinking, and brain shrinkage. In the body, damage has been done to the liver, heart, lungs, kidney, GI tract, pancreas, and the immune system. This downward spiral results in shame, depression, anxiety, paranoia, and other mental disorders.

It may sound hopeless for those addicted to substances, but recovery centers do offer hope. Some of the most successful centers are the Adult and Teen Challenge Centers which provide Christian guidance to the participants. By sharing the love of God, the participants begin their long journey towards redemption and recovery. The brain may recover, but much time and enormous effort are required for it to do so.

Excessive eating of foods high in carbohydrates (sugars) and fats and even excessive coffee, (caffeine, a simulate) or artificial food additives, can affect the brain and body almost like illegal drugs do. Even though keeping our body fit is commendable, endorphins, and other feel good chemicals could lead to dependence. Now the experts say our use of electronic devices are leading to addictive behaviors, excreting the same chemicals in order to feel good. Addictive behaviors become the compelling drive in the individual's life and take a toll on our financial status and relationships. The old adage, "Everything in moderation," still stands in regards to or eating food as well as our behaviors (Hesiod, *Moderation*).

Our bodies cannot tolerate the constant artificial "highs" without hitting a wall. So, why do we search for the elusive high? Is it the desire of our heart to fill the void that was left when Adam sinned? The promise of eternally "feel good" feelings can only be fulfilled in one identity, Jesus Christ! Jesus does not force us to love and worship Him. Jesus does not control our lives without our permission! He gives us free will. Mind altering substances, false gods, dictators, controlling relationships, and ideologies control our lives without our permission! We can live in freedom and trust His pure, absolute love which gives us His peace and joy. He set guidelines for our lives, not to cramp our joy and happiness, but to make lasting joy and happiness possible! That is the beauty of our Lord! If you have committed your life to Jesus, these guidelines are for you! If you have not committed your life to Him, the guidelines may seem unloving, constraining, and irrelevant!

The body makes many powerful direct demands on our being and needs to be in subjection to our regenerated spirit and soul. If not, Satan gains access to our being through the evil desires of our bodies as well as our unregenerate soul. Talk to your body, give it commands on what it is allowed to demand! You do this automatically without realizing you are doing it. When the alarm goes off, you may say to yourself, "What time is it?" or "I am not getting up yet!" When dieting, "I do not need that extra dessert." Sometimes we say, "I know I do not need dessert, but I am going to eat it anyway." Your **will** just submit to your **body!** It is helpful to say, "Yes, I do want it, but I am not willing to gain back the weight I have struggled to lose!" Remembering the pain of losing weight may deter the desire. Answer the flesh with a resounding answer that is coupled with consequences, like "I will have to buy a larger size or I am going to be less attractive." Of course, the best option is to pray and allow the Lord to help you control your desire to overeat. So speak to it! Tell your body it is not hungry and does not need the extra food. The body usually will comply if you really mean it.

The sexual drive is another powerful influence on our being that requires submission to God's guidance. The sex drive is another direct demand the body makes on our being. It was

God's idea to design the man and woman with the capability of reproduction as well as being able to parent their little ones in a safe and healthy environment.

As already noted, a healthy control of the mind, will, and emotions, (the soul) will guide us in making Godly decisions when facing strong sexual impulses. A sexual relationship within the confines of marriage is a precious gift for the couples' enjoyment and fulfillment. Marriage seals the love, devotion, and intimacy between the two as the two become one. The Bible has much to say on this topic. During creation, God looked at all creation and declared that it was good six times! The first time it was "not good" came in Genesis 2:18: The Lord God said, "It is not good for the man to be alone. I will make a helper suitable for him." That is where intimacy is shared mirroring the love and intimacy of the Father. It has been said, marriage takes three, the man, the wife and Heavenly Father in the center.

Violating the commitment to fidelity inflicts intense pain on both partners. Also, if the bonds of marriage are forsaken 1 Corinthians 6:16 warns: "And don't you realize that if a man joins himself to a prostitute he becomes one body with her. For the Scriptures say, 'They are united into one.'" Sexual impulses are more difficult to control because there is the influence of another person. In a premarital situation, a discussion with your partner concerning your values and convictions about premarital sex will promote more restraint on both partners. If one is not willing to comply, then it is not a balanced relationship!

The Apostle Paul gave these guidelines to the early Christians about sexual immorality and its impact on the physical body. God wants us to enjoy the life He has given to us. 1Corinthians 6:15 NLT: "Don't you realize that your bodies are actually part of Christ? Should a man take his body, which is part of Christ, and join it to a prostitute? Never!" And in verse 18: "Run from sexual sin! No other sin so clearly affects the body as this one does. For sexual immorality is a sin against your own body." The Christians are further warned in Romans 1:25: "Even the women turned against the natural way to have sex and instead indulged in sex with each other." And in verse 27: "And the men, instead of having normal sexual relations with women, burned with lust with each other. Men did shameful things with other men, and as a result of this sin, they suffered within themselves the penalty they deserved." Paul knew the Creator God knew what was best for His creation! After all, He created us and gave us His owner's manual, the Bible, as guidance.

What can we do if we are committing sexual sins that have such a negative impact on our physical body? Call out to Jesus for help! Jesus hears the cry for help and He will answer you and show you what to do. He will never ask you to do something that is impossible, but will equip you to do the impossible in Him and by Him! Rely on Jesus to make His changes in your life and He will!

The Lord is an infinite divine designer. Our bodies are unique and come in all shapes, sizes, and shades of color. In the USA, each of us is probably of a mixture of races and I am one of those. Having had a DNA test performed, it determined I am a mixture of five! None of this surprised me as I have felt a commonality with most people groups. We know our fingerprints are all different from each other even in identical twins. Consider how many people that have lived, are living now, infants not yet born and infants that did not make it to birth; that is a lot of designs! Perhaps our Lord wanted to show His infinite love to each of us by creating us with our own unique design. That is true physically as well as in our personality. No two people are alike! Does that not make you feel special? It should!

Accepting one's own physical attributes is imperative for a healthy self-image. Realizing the extent our Creator went to make us so individually unique should make us comfortable with who we are. Yet often we complain about our appearance. Why is that? Somehow Satan tries to divert us from being what our Creator intended us to be. If Satan can't steal our image by allowing the entrance of low self-esteem or insecurity, he will inflate our ego by allowing pride, arrogance, and narcissism to rule our personality. Let us be thankful to Jesus for how He created us. We can be confident of who we are because it is He who has made us and all our abilities and accomplishments are because of Him! This is the attitude of humility.

The beauty of the body is its ability to recover from most invasive events. As you see, it's difficult to separate the spirit, soul, and body. The effects of one affects the other. The strength is their unity.

"Hey, I Am In Here!"

Ms. Williams, an elderly unconscious lady, was admitted to ICU with a CT diagnosis of a massive intracerebral bleed. Although she had a heartbeat, she was totally dependent on a ventilator for breathing and multiple IV medications to support her blood pressure. The neurological checks showed no response to stimuli. Later that morning, I was giving her a bath and I was quietly singing to her. All of a sudden, I sensed she heard me! "Ms. Williams, I think you can hear me. If you can hear me please, blink your eyes once for "yes" and twice for "no"." Her response was one slight blink! Wow! Then, I asked her if she knew what had happened to her, two blinks! I told her what day it was and what had happened to her. She indicated she understood with one blink. After communicating with her with eye blinks, I explained to her family our system for communication. They were so excited! They spent the day communicating with her with eye blinks!

This condition is known as "Locked-in Syndrome." The person experiences total paralysis of all body movements except for eye blinking and heart beats. This occurs in 1% of all strokes, there is no cure, no treatment except complete life support. Most die before reaching the hospital due to the respiratory arrest. If they make it to the hospital and are put on life support, the expected survival rate is just a few days. There is one gentleman on record who did survive this kind of stroke. He said he knew everything going on around him, his thinking was totally intact and he even had periods of awake and sleep. Not being able to communicate with others and hearing the medical staff discussing his dismal situation with his wife was unbearable. "Hey, I'm in here." he screamed to himself. He was quite frustrated until someone noticed his eyes blinking. This is one reason why we remind all staff and family to be cautious of what they say in the presence of an unconscious patient! The hearing is the last thing to go! This is an example of the *body*'s inability to perform and the spirit and soul completely alert and aware. What a total feeling of hopelessness!

Ms. Williams's family were wonderful to work with us. She had informed them earlier that she did not want extraordinary measures taken at the end of life and had a living will. She was ready to die, having lived many years in the presence of her Lord. The physician came in and talked with the family and to the patient. It was determined with her consent to discontinue life support later.

She enjoyed another day but when I asked her about the life support decision, I did not get a reply. "Am I not asking the right question?" One blink. "Okay. I will keep asking." After asking a few questions, I figured out what she wanted. She did not want to be aware when the ventilator was discontinued. We reminded her that she would be sedated and would not be aware when the ventilator was discontinued. She seemed relieved and wanted to see her family once again before she went to sleep. Our hearts were broken, but we felt good that her last hours had been filled with joy and peace.

No Return!

Revelation 22:12:
Behold, I am coming soon! My reward is with me, and I will give to everyone according to what he has done."

Pastor Shepard:

In the late 1960's, Pastor Shepard, a 53 year old man, had not been feeling well over the past several hours and finally decided go to his physician. He was in the waiting room when his condition became worse. He stood to notify the secretary when he passed out; the paramedics delivered him to the Emergency Department where oxygen, IV fluids, and initial medications were given, EKG, X-ray, and labs, were completed. He was very cheerful, pain free, and even joking with me upon his arrival to ICU. He stated he did not need to be in the hospital much less ICU. We were finishing his admission and I was assuring him he was correct in seeking help.

About two hours passed when he complained of slight nausea when he saw the liquid diet ordered for him which was routine for suspected myocardial Infarction. "I am not really that sick, you just need patients," he teased. Our census was low that evening.

His relaxed demeanor suddenly changed with a sharp, non-relenting chest pain, nausea and vomiting. His tan complexion was now pale and he was diaphoretic. His heart rate and blood pressure had increased momentarily with no change in his monitor pattern. His pain and nausea were relieved somewhat with medication, but he was very lethargic. The monitor pattern was beginning to show signs of an evolving inferior wall myocardial infarction with intermittent first degree heart block. His physician was notified. I knew his condition was grave, my heart was broken, but I knew I could not give in to my emotions or let my concern show. We prayed a short prayer together and the medication he had received had relived most of his pain. I quietly reminded God that he was too young to be this condition.

In the1970's and 1980's much attention was given to improving cardiac care. Coronary artery bypass graft surgeries brought hope to those affected with coronary artery disease. The ability to do cardiac interventions for coronary occlusions through cardiac catheterizations has changed the treatment for many. Implantable devices to control cardiac dysrhythmias have become common. When one considers the advances in cardiovascular care in the last 50 years, it is amazing! Unfortunately, we did not have those interventions available for Pastor Shepard in the late 1960's.

Pastor Shepard's pain was increasing again; this time his blood pressure was dropping. In an instant he had a cardiac arrest. A code was called. I was doing chest compressions and others were providing breaths via bag valve mask. The physician had come and other medications were given to stabilize his heart rhythm.

After the defibrillation, Pastor Shepard's regained consciousness almost instantly.

He opened his eyes and seemed astonished to see me. "What are you doing in my bed?" he asked. I was standing on a stool in order to reach his chest to do compressions and did not have time to get down off the stool before he saw me! I explained what I was doing and he just smiled and nodded.

When things were more settled, he indicated he wanted to tell me something. "I want you to know when I died I saw Jesus. He had his arms opened wide and was waiting for me. The next time I go, I am not coming back!" He was so matter of fact about it, no fear or dread, just peace and a smile.

This was the first time I had experienced anything like this in my five years of nursing even though I had performed cardiac resuscitation several times. At this time I had not heard of Near Death Experiences. A more experienced nurse was with me and she just reacted as if it were normal. We both had heard people talk about seeing loved ones on "the other side." but I thought that was due to hallucinations, delusions, or medication. That is what I was being told.

A short time later, Pastor Shepard had another cardiac arrest. This time we were unable to resuscitate him. He had slipped from this realm into the waiting arms of Jesus! My heart was broken, but I knew he was rejoicing in heaven.

Many years later, the Lord permitted me to share with Pastor Shepard's family member what happened that day. I was so young and inexperienced with Near Death Experiences, I did not know or understand that the Near Death Experience was a valid experience. Since that time, I have been more open and I encourage my patients to be also. Many are hesitant to tell the nurse or their family of their experience. They may think no one will understand. That is changing as Near Death Experiences are getting more exposure.

What I learned from Pastor Shepard was how peaceful one can be in the face of death. He was really calm before and after the arrest, no anxiousness. He had been doing life as usual that day, probably with no thought of death, and yet, he faced it as if it were routine. Perhaps that is the way he lived. It made me evaluate my life. I am not sure I am there yet, because there is so much I want to do; so many others I want to know this love of our marvelous Lord and Savior.

Peter 5:6-7. "Humble yourselves, therefore, under God's mighty hand, that he may lift you up in due time. Cast all your anxiety on him because he cares for you."

Near Death and Dying

As stated earlier, patients can hear often even if they appear to be totally unconscious. Case in point, after recovery from a cardiac arrest, a gentleman declared to me he was going to rewrite his will when he got out of the hospital. He heard his two sons in a heated discussion concerning his possessions while they thought he was unconscious. I don't know what happened later but I do hope the family resolved the situation through love and forgiveness.

Another such case involved a healthcare provider who stated the patient would be a "vegetable" if he survived. I was closer to the patient and I thought perhaps the noise of the ventilator would prevent the patient from hearing the statement. Not only did he recover from his head injury, he was able to walk out of the hospital! And yes, he let the healthcare provider know he was not a vegetable! It is an easy mistake to make because all of your senses are telling you the patient is unaware, but please remember, hearing takes so little effort and it is the last sense to go.

There are many lessons we learn in working with the near death or with the dying. Some will think this topic is depressing, but dying is just as much a part of living as anything else. To me, dying is just a transition from one state to another. When these mortal bodies become worn out or diseased, death can be a welcomed transition. I have had the privilege to be at the bedside of the dying and hold their hand, to pray a prayer as they make the transition. There is nothing more satisfying than to see a grimace of pain or uncertainty turn into a peaceful countenance. I have heard the dying say, "Do you hear that beautiful music?" Or they make reference to seeing a "light" or meeting a loved one "on the other side." Some simply take their last breath peacefully, while a few scream in horror as they transition from this life to the next.

Another man who experienced a near death experience was definitely excited about it. I was not with him during his experience but his description was similar to the others. He told about the incredible love and total acceptance he felt and of course the beautiful flowers, colors, and music. He felt compelled to tell his physician but hesitated thinking it may not be appropriate. I assured him it would be okay and told him I would be with him when he did so. The physician had a beautiful response. Looking across the bed to me he said, "Praise the Lord." The patient had not expected that and neither did I!

I have had the privilege of talking to believers after a Near Death Experience. Most of them agree the experience removes all fear of death! That should be an encouragement to all of us who are on this side of death. But what about the non-believers? I can not say for all but I have heard of some who did not have a heavenly experience.

One man said he had such an experience and he had never talked about it nor would he because it was too frightening. A man on television told his experience of being in hell. He describes how "evil beings" were tearing at his clothes and his body to inflict pain. There was another man who I believe had such an encounter. I was not with him when he had a cardiac arrest but I was there the day after the arrest. Prior to the arrest, he was angry, cursing the physicians, nurses and everyone else, including his family. After his arrest, he stopped cursing and would just look around the unit as if he were afraid of something or someone. He was still very quiet when he was transferred from the unit.

Near Death Experiences may happen more than we know. The person may not wish to tell it or they may not remember when it happens. But what happens when they do not return to earth, is that they die.

Grief brings a whole host of emotions and does an impact upon the body and mind. To lose someone we love is to feel a loss of intimacy, loss of communication, and loss of fellowship with the person. The deeper we loved the person, the greater the loss we feel. The sorrow, sadness, pain, and heartache has the potential to almost paralyze our being.

Inability to sleep or mentally focus, loss of appetite, shock, depression and loneliness are symptoms of grief. As unpleasant grief is, it is a normal reaction to a loss.

Part of the pain from grief may be related to what we did not express, forgiveness not given, or regret for time not spent with him/her while he/she was living. "Could I have done things differently?" Guilt, self blame, and anger only intensifies the emotions we feel during grief. Do not just deny grief and expect it to go away. We know Jesus can handle all our griefs and sorrows. The Lord can heal all the places in our hearts where we agonize over guilt, blame, or our lack of forgiveness.

It is best to forgive the person while he/she still lives, but I have known people who forgave on the grave of the offender! Case in point; a lady I know who received great comfort in forgiving her childhood sexual molester after his death. At last, she was free of the bondage of what he had done to her. But we may think he was the one who should have asked her for forgiveness. Nevertheless, in the Lord's Prayer, Jesus simply said "And forgive us our debts, as as we forgive out debtors." Matthew 6:12. KJV. And In Matthew 6:14-15. NLT. Jesus goes on to explain: "If you forgive those who sin against you, your Heavenly Father will forgive you. But if you refuse to forgive others, your Father will not forgive your sins." That is a strong statement and should not be taken lightly! Dear Father, is there anyone that I need to forgive? If so, I choose to do so now! This is the kind of prayer He is waiting and wanting to answer.

Forgiveness requires grace. By God's grace which is God's unmerited favor, He forgave me. Since I could not earn forgiveness for my sin, how can I withhold forgiveness from others? This is how I can now forgive like Jesus does!

It definitely does not have to be death that brings grief. Loss of a marriage, friendship, job, or even a pet may bring grief to the surface. Likewise, grief may come due to an altered body image such as an amputation of a limb or inability to function physically. This type of loss is a devastating blow to any person. My work in a burn unit taught me how difficult it is for a person to accept a new scarred image of themselves. From a small child to a pretty twenty-one year old young lady, or an eighty year old man to name a few were afflicted with this pain both physically and psychologically. Again, the Lord's comfort is always available and greatly needed for this type of grieving.

Experts agree there are five to seven stages to the grieving process. Each person works through the stages in his/her own way and, more importantly, in his/her own time. Starting with shock, denial, anger, guilt, bargaining, and then hopefully working to some kind of acceptance are some of the stages (Kessler, *The Five*). The grieving need to avoid numbing agents such as excessive alcohol or drugs. Support groups and counseling are beneficial to the grieving and may be required to work through the pain.

What do I say to the grieving? I've learned to simply sit with them after being told of the death of their loved one, listen to them, or even cry with them. Never say "I know how you feel," or "I lost my mom recently." That is not what they need to hear! Especially when the death is current. They do not have the emotional stamina to hear about your trauma, nor do they want to hear. Be kind, considerate, and express genuine love for their situation by saying something like: "I'm so sorry for your loss," "I sense you loved him/her very much," or " I'll be thinking and praying for you in this difficult time," or "May I pray for you now?" If the griever is alone, the touch of your hand on his/her hand may be appropriate and reassuring or even a hug may be appropriate and reassuring if he/she is totally distraught. Use wisdom here. The prayer doesn't have to be elaborate, just thank Jesus for the life of the person and ask Jesus for comfort and peace.

As Christians, we do not grieve as others do. 1Thessalonians 4:13: "Brothers, we do not want you to be ignorant about those who fall asleep, or to grieve like the rest of men, who have no hope." We grieve, yes, but we have hope in life after death for ourselves and our loved ones. We have learned to trust our Father, knowing His comfort and peace, is available for us if we ask. When we do not understand our world or it seems unfair, Jesus is always waiting to help us with our pain whether it is within our emotional, mental, or social realm. We must choose to think about God's attributes: His all knowing wisdom, knowledge, power, and endless love for us. Then we may give Him thanks and praise for the hope, comfort, and love He gives. Grief teaches us to trust in God's compassion.

Trust in the Lord!

As never before in my life time, it is imperative to learn to trust in the Lord. We are entering an age of uncertainty in our society. Everything we think is normal has been challenged and shaken. I suppose those that were living in Europe during World War II felt the same about their future. As we try to make sense of what is going on, we can be sure our Lord is still in charge! Nothing takes Him by surprise! God never has to say, "Well I never thought about that," or "I never thought the people would do that!" The world is showing us that to have hope we must place it in God's loving, faithful care.

The United States has been in a stupor for years. We have forgotten who we are and what we were called to be. Our morals are no more. Now we have two choices: repent for our sins or lose our country. Whatever happens, God is still in charge! He will not allow His plan for His creation to fail. This time may be a time of pruning and cleansing. We each need to do that! Do not let a spirit of fear enter in our souls, as fear can be paralyzing. Fear obliterates our faith. Satan's favorite tool is fear; faith in God will break the yoke of fear. Proverbs 3:4-5 Amp: "Lean on, trust in, and be confident in the Lord with all your heart and mind; do not rely on your own insight or understanding. In all your ways know, recognize, and acknowledge Him, and He will direct and make straight and plain your paths." You can trust Him, just do not forget who God is.

Father God is so magnificent in all His ways. How does man comprehend all of God? Every aspect of His being is more than we can fathom. Even the depths of the ocean has not been fully explored and understood. Contrast that with outer space. Sure we have been to the moon and our rover has been to Mars. But that is only a speck of His creation. How about the universe and beyond, ever expanding. Our

Lord, in His Holiness, has allowed us a glimpse into His magnificent ways. What is beyond this "glimpse"? With each generation He has revealed a new facet of His being. There is nothing too big, too small, or too insignificant to have His attention!

As a child, I had a concept of God and Jesus, as many children do. I knew someone was with me. I sensed His love and protection. As I grew older, my concept grew. Then there came a day, July 23, 1953, when I felt the Holy Spirit dealing with me to commit my heart to Jesus. My dad kneeled and prayed the sinner's prayer with me at the altar! Suddenly, the heavy lump of conviction left my throat and I felt free, loved, and complete. If you are not sure you have made that commitment, you must invite Jesus into your heart with a simple prayer now.

In my early twenties, I was not as close to the Lord as I was earlier in life. I slowly permitted other things to occupy my attention and affections. I was working swing shifts and had little time for consistent Bible reading, prayer, and fellowship with my Father. It did not happen overnight. I was miserable, until I accidentally ran into an old friend. She grabbed my arm as she said, "Now I know what you were telling me about when we were in nursing school. My husband and I have given our hearts to the Lord and Jesus has baptized us in the Holy Spirit!" My head was spinning! I had told her about Jesus earlier and now she was unaware she was witnessing to me! The joy and enthusiasm in her life was what I was missing without being aware. That week I returned to Jesus; He was waiting for me and He baptized me in the Holy Spirit! What a powerful event that was! I never knew how beneficial it would be to walk in the Spirit of God. All one has to do is to ask Jesus to baptize you in His precious Holy Spirit just like you asked Him to come into your heart. How precious our Lord was to send someone to me to meet a need that I did not know was there. That is His love and faithfulness! How great is our God!

A few years ago, we were privileged to visit Mt. Graham International Observatory, one of the largest astrophysical research sites in the world, located in Southeast Arizona. The Observatory houses two Large Binocular Telescopes which permit astronomers to observe the faintest and most distant objects in the universe. It is almost more than the mind can fathom how eminently vast space is. And "God created the heavens" became so surreal to me! To be able to see the multiple galaxies beyond ours was quite an experience. We, with the psalmist David, say: "When I consider your heavens, the work of your fingers, the moon and the stars, which You have set in place, what is man that You are mindful of him, the son of man that You care for him?" Psalm 8:3 WOW!

From the vastness of the universe down to the complexity of a human cell, not to mention the microscopic organisms that are here among us show us His glory. When we think of God, our minds cannot comprehend His magnificent being or His ways. The only thing I know is, He loves and cares for us as demonstrated by His ultimate gift of Jesus Christ who gave His life to free us from sin by His death on the cross. God's desire for a relationship with us is beyond my comprehension, but He demonstrated His desire for us and His Word proves it. It is truly a privilege to know our Heavenly Father intimately. He is a good, good God! So, who are we?

We are a spirit, first of all, we have a soul and we live in a body. The spirit is the essence of who we are; the soul makes up the rest of our non-tangible being such as the way we think, act, and feel. The body houses the spirit and soul. Because the three are so integrated, it is difficult to separate them into three entities. Yet, the three are so different in their scope of actions. It reminds me of what Genesis says: "Let us" (Father, Son, Holy Spirit) "make man in our image, male and female He made us." God is triune. Man is made in His triune image-spirit, soul and body. Man desperately needs the Spirit of God to be merged with his/her spirit so his/her spirit can be controlled by God. Then his/her controlled spirit can control his/her soul; the mind, will, and emotions which will help control his/her body as well as the way he/she behaves. Our ultimate desire is for us to move through our lives with Him inside of us, as well as beside, behind and in front of us. His perfect plan cannot be thwarted by mere man. For that, I am glad!

Have I convinced you of God's existence? God has a plan for your life. God loves you unconditionally; His profound desire is to communicate with you via His Spirit to your spirit, now and throughout eternity! Have I convince you of your need to put your faith and trust in Him? I do hope so!

I Thessalonians 5:23-24:
Now may the God of peace make you holy in every way, and may your whole spirit and soul and body be kept blameless until our Lord Jesus Christ comes again. God will make this happen, for he who call you is faithful.

Notes:

- ## Chapter One: When It Started

Preventing Workplace Violence: A Road Map for Healthcare Facilities. December 2015, https://www.osha.gov.

Collins, Heather M.S., C.G.C., Calro, Sheri, RN, M.S. and Morrison, Stephanie, M.P.H. *Precision Medicine Information Needs in the Precision Era*, April 2016, https://www.ncbl.nim.nih.gov

Hsieh, Chih-Hsiang, *Application of Non Invasive Low Strength Pulse Electric Field to EGCG Treatment*, December 2017, https://www.ncbl.nim.nih.gov

Brigham Heath Hub, *Using Sound Wave to Treat a Wide Spectrum of Disease*, January, 2020. https://wwwbrigmanheathhub.com

- ## Chapter Eight: The Spirit

Lindsey, Hal, "*Man can live about 40 days without food, about three days without water, about 8 minutes without air, but only for one second without hope."* Goodreads quotes: 103469. https://www. goodreads.com/quotes

Lewis, C.S. *Four Greek words for love in the Bible,* Wikipedia- https://www.en.m.wikipedia.org

- ## Chapter Eleven: The Soul

Phillips, Steve. *The Mystery in the Chata and Pesha: Hebrew Words for Sin, Chattah, Awon, Pesha. March 31, 2018* https://www.livingwordin3d.com

Brown, Lauretta, *Margaret Sanger Wasn't Just a Racist-She Also Targeted Disabled People* National Catholic Register July 30, 2020. https://www. en.m.Wikipedia.org

- ## Chapter Twelve: The Mind

Brain Basics: Know Your Brain, Bethesda, MD, The National Institute of Neurological Disorders and Stroke. https://www.ninds.nih.gov

Wilken, Patrick MD, *Freud's Model of the Human Mind,* Journal Psyche, Est 1992, https://www. journalpsyche.org

Wilken, Patrick MD, *Freud's Model of the Human Mind,* Journal Psyche, Est 1992, https://www. journalpsyche.org

Habit Formation: How the 20/90 Rule Helps You Build Good Habits and a Better Life. https://www. capespace.com

Wilken, Patrick MD, *Freud's Model of the Human Mind,* Journal Psyche, Est 1992, https://www. journalpsyche.org

Sleep Cycle - A Language, Neuroscience of Sleep, https://www.enWikipedia.org

Sleep Cycle-A Language, Neuroscience of Sleep, https:// www.en.Wikipedia.org

Wilken, Patrick MD, *Freud's Model of the Human Mind,* Journal Psyche, Est. 1992, https://www.journaldpsyche.org

Einstein Albert > Quotes Goodreads: Books Reviews 2020 https://www.goodreads.com

Porter, Jane,*The Neuroscience of Imagination,* 2013, Fast Company, https:// www.fastcompany.com

Beauty Is In the Eyes of the Beholder Synonyms With Definition. Macmillan Thesaurus https://macmillanthesarus.com

Mental Health Information Statistics, title *Transforming the Understanding and Treatment of Mental Illness,* April 2019, https://www.nih.gov

COVID 19, Pandemic and Suicide Ideation, June 2020, https://www.cdc.gov.

• ## Chapter Fourteen: The Emotions

Pullman Jill, COT, *Three Types of Tears,* Cleveland Eye Clinic, July 16, 2019, https://wwwclevelandeyeclinic.com

Pope, Alexander, *An Essay on Criticism, quote "To Err is Human, to Forgive, Divine".* Dictionary.com

Bortschiller, Jake, *Staying Safe Around Bears,* April 13,2018, https://www.nps.gov

Habit Formation How the 20/90 Rule Helps You Build Good Habits and a Better Life, https://www.cape space.com

Lewis, C.S. *Four Greek words for love in the Bible,* Wikipedia- https://www.en.m.wikipedia.org

Lewis, C.S. *Four Greek words for love in the Bible,* Wikipedia- https://www.en.m.wikipedia.org

Lewis, C.S. *Four Greek words for love in the Bible,* Wikipedia- https://www.en.m.wikipedia.org

- ## Chapter Fifteen:

Does a Laugh per Day Keep the Doctor Away? March 31, 2017, https://www.uspn.com

Miller, Michael, MD, and Fry, William, MD, *The Effects of Mirthful Laughter on the Human Cardiovascular System,* November 2009, https://www.ncbi. nim.nih.gov

WhyQuit- https://www.WhyQuit.com

Hesiod (c.700 bc) *"Moderation in All Things,"* Oxford Reference, https://www.oxfordreference.com

- ## Chapter Eighteen: Near Death and Dying

Kessler, David *The Five Stages of Grief, Remembering the Love, Releasing the Pain,* https://www.grief.com

Scripture Index
(chronological order)

Matthew 5:44-45a

I John 4:7-8, 19

I Corinthians 13:4-7

Galatians 6:22

John 15:12-13

Psalms 34:18

Jeremiah 29:13

Matthew 7:7-8

Psalms 19:1 (NLT)

II Timothy. 1:7

Proverbs 20:27

John 16:33

John 3:3-7

Hebrews 10:16-18

I Corinthians 2:9-12

John 10:27

Mark 4:35-40

Mark 9:22-24

James 1:5 (NLT)

Psalms 139:23

Isaiah 9:16 (NLT)

II Thessalonians 2:10

John 10:27

Romans 1:8

Proverbs 22:6

Matthew 7:20

Isaiah 54:13

Malachi 3:11

I Corinthians 15:42

Luke 9:1

Mark 11:12

Mark 11:20

Psalms 116:15

Psalms 117:2

II Thessalonians 3:5

III John 1:2

Psalms 103:1-3

Psalms 51:1-2

Hebrews 12:1 (NLT)

Hebrews 10:16

John 10:10b

Psalms 100:4

Luke 16:19-31

Proverbs 23:7

Genesis 3:5b

Hebrews 9:27a

I Peter 5:8 (KJV)

Ecclesiastes 1:9

I Corinthians 13:12 (KJV)

Hebrews 11:3

II Corinthians 10:5 (KJV)

Mark 7:20-23

Genesis 6:5-6

II Samuel chapter 11

Psalms 119:37

I Samuel 16:14-23

II Timothy 4:3 (NLT)

Psalms 34:8 (NLT)

Psalms 119:10

Romans 12:2-3

Acknowledgments

To my Lord Jesus Christ for giving me the strength, encouragement, words, and Scriptures to complete this work. All glory to Him!

To all the precious people in my life, thank you! Some of you have encouraged me when I wanted to quit, some gave me needed advice, and others added value to the manuscript by correcting errors!

To my wonderful pastors who have taught and lead me in God's ways. Your wisdom, knowledge, and influence have been valuable to my spiritual growth.

To my husband, daughters, Beth and Lora, and family for their understanding, encouragement, and patience through the three years of writing. And to my friend and editor Gail Williamson who stuck with me through it all, lovingly correcting my mistakes.

To my editors, protect managers, publishers, and designers, my gratitude for making this possible and readable at Salem Author Service and to Xulon Press: Danielle Sarta and all her team.

About the Author

My Calling began as a desire to help suffering people. Later, I realized people needed help within their spirit and soul as well as their body. The stories I shared made me realize I was responsible for sharing Jesus with the dying. I praise God for that opportunity.

The nursing profession has many facets, none of them boring, and an opportunity to constantly learn. No matter how many changes there have been, the scope of care by an empathetic nurse has never changed.

To the young nurse I say, "You will face challenges, but you will find fulfillment, joy, and pride in your profession!"

My experience in nursing became personal to me almost 30 years ago. I was diagnosed with stage 2 breast cancer. Our Lord enveloped me in such an unbelievable bubble of peace that I could not be anxious! All praises and thankfulness to Jesus!

Then the disease reoccurred 7 years ago. Chemotherapy, surgery, and radiation were done again for stage 4 breast cancer. I was given 3 months without treatment, or one year with treatment! I chose the latter. Then, 4 years ago, a small tumor in the brain fractured and caused two strokes. Through it all, Jesus has never failed me once! The Lord's supernatural peace, deep love, and fellowship are always with me. He has blessed me with a wonderful, loving husband and daughters, as my support system, and has extended my life seven years!

Serving the Lord Jesus has been a most fulfilling adventure and one of my greatest joys. Whether in the role as a wife, mother, nurse, a role as an instructor for the Master's Commission (our Bible College), or on the mission field, I am truly thankful to God for allowing me to be a part of His call.

Our society has many ways to maneuver through life, but my walk with God has been tried and true. Get to know the Father, learn to hear His voice, and obey His instructions! Our Father God is just waiting to have a relationship and conversation with you! Get ready, Jesus is coming soon!

CPSIA information can be obtained
at www.ICGtesting.com
Printed in the USA
BVHW050131140721
611841BV00012B/1045